1990

SUICIDE

Contemporary Issues in Philosophy

Series Editors: Robert M. Baird
Stuart E. Rosenbaum

Other titles in this series:

*The Ethics of Abortion:
Pro-Life vs. Pro-Choice*
edited by Robert M. Baird
and Stuart E. Rosenbaum

Euthanasia: The Moral Issues
edited by Robert M. Baird
and Stuart E. Rosenbaum

Morality and the Law
edited by Robert M. Baird
and Stuart E. Rosenbaum

Philosophy of Punishment
edited by Robert M. Baird
and Stuart E. Rosenbaum

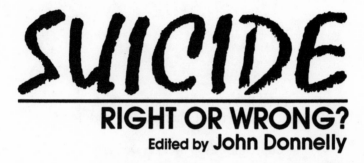

SUICIDE

RIGHT OR WRONG?

Edited by John Donnelly

Contemporary Issues in Philosophy

PROMETHEUS BOOKS
BUFFALO, NEW YORK

Published 1990 by Prometheus Books
700 East Amherst Street, Buffalo, New York 14215

Copyright © 1990 by John Donnelly

Library of Congress Cataloging-in-Publication Data

Suicide : right or wrong? / edited by John Donnelly.
     p.   cm. — (Contemporary issues in philosophy)
  Includes bibliographical references.
  ISBN 0-87975-595-4 (alk. paper)
   1. Suicide—Moral and ethical aspects. I. Donnelly, John.
II. Series.
HV6545.S8426   1990
179′.7—dc20   89-70302
                                                          CIP

Printed on acid-free paper in the United States of America

Contents

PART TWO: WHEN DO WE CALL IT SUICIDE?

PART THREE: IS SUICIDE MORAL? IS IT RATIONAL?

Introduction

"There is but one truly serious philosophical problem, and that is suicide. Judging whether life is or is not worth living amounts to answering the fundamental question of philosophy."

—Albert Camus

"Whoever is oppressed with the burden of life, whoever desires life and affirms it, but abhors its torments, such a man has no deliverance to hope from death, and cannot right himself by suicide."

—Arthur Schopenhauer

"Free to die and free in death, able to say a holy No when the time for Yes has passed; thus he knows how to die and to live."

—Friedrich Nietzsche

The topic of suicide is emotionally wrenching; it can arouse great wrath as well as considerable sorrow for those who have been affected by it. We often have understandable pity for the oppressed, the miserable, and the downtrodden who, because of their respective misfortunes in life, resort to suicide; and considerable anger for those persons who are whimsical and frivolous perpetrators. Yet calm, rational reflection seems called for, especially since it is probably true that all of us, however fleetingly, entertain the thought of suicide in our hearts at some point.

The reality of suicide knows no demographic boundary. It occurs in all cultures, nationalities, races, age-groups, and professions. Suicide rates appear relatively high in Finland, Hungary, West Germany, and among

American Indians, college-age students, and psychiatrists. Where the bonds of family and socio-economic cohesion are fragile, evidence suggests a higher incidence of suicide, whether among the childless, the divorced, the widowed, the unemployed, the dispossessed, the alienated, the emotionally distraught, substance abusers, or whomever.[1]

Theories abound regarding the conditions that influence people in their decision to commit suicide. Some insist that it results from a biochemical imbalance (e.g., low serotonin levels in individuals suffering from depression), while others cling to psychoanalytic explanations, socio-cultural influences, and a whole host of other psycho-social-biological variables. At the present time, no theory has risen above the rest. Obviously, any mortality table that suggests suicide is not widely practiced would be considered deceptive. The United States Center for Health Statistics doesn't list a death as suicide unless there is proof that it was *intentional*, i.e., premeditated— a condition all the more difficult to establish given the paucity of suicide notes. Along with the fact that suicide is frequently underreported, euphemisms proliferate to soften the harshness of what the philosopher Immanuel Kant termed "the intention to destroy oneself." Indeed, intimations of suicide can appear "magical" and "consoling." Nietzsche said "by means of it one gets successfully through many a bad night."

The situation of the would-be suicide is notoriously ambivalent. It isn't death that is so devoutly wished for, as it is relief from physical pain and/or mental anguish. There are suicide prevention centers in over 200 cities in the United States. The fact that so many people seek help at such centers strongly suggests that they are looking for a solution to their respective plights.

Surprisingly, suicide occurs at an alarming rate among the young, persons supposedly in the prime of their lives. Adolescent suicide in the United States rose by 300 percent in the twenty years between 1955 and 1975, and has stabilized somewhat since. Unfortunately, approximately 18 teenagers kill themselves every day in this country; and every hour about 57 adolescents unsuccessfully attempt self-engineered death. Much higher rates of teen suicide are reported in Switzerland and Austria. Only car accidents cause more deaths among adolescents than suicide, and many of these may well be "autocides." Yet despite a number of recent federal, state, and local programs attempting to address this problem, suicide remains a taboo subject for many parents. Sons and daughters may die by their own hands, but the deaths are rationalized as Russian Roulette gone awry, accidental poisoning, or attributed to alcohol or drug abuse.

Nonetheless, studies indicate that most teen suicides occur in the home, usually during early evening when parents are close by. Experts view such suicides as desperate pleas for love and attention, or spiteful acts of revenge. Yet, critics of suicide education programs in our schools claim the statistical data are skewed, and accuse suicidologists of seeking to hawk their theories for personal gain and publicity. Critics contend that such programs would inadvertently serve to increase the number of suicides as they heighten public awareness.

In 1987, the U.S. Department of Health and Human Services reported some 12.7 deaths by suicide per 100,000 population in this country (13.1 in 1986). In 1985, some 4,760 people between the ages of 15 and 24 committed suicide in the United States. On a global level, there are approximately 400,000 suicides annually. Of course, millions of people unsuccessfully attempt suicide every year. Males seem to commit suicide more often than females and by more violent means. However, women attempt suicide more frequently than men. Doubtless, these figures are statistically inaccurate, inasmuch as respect for the dead and the deceased's family often influence physicians (when officially certifying the death) to list genuine suicides as deaths by some other cause. The practice of euphemistic coroners' reports has often reached peaks of morbid, if not comical, absurdity, as in the case of a British report that described the "accidental" death of a man who just happened to shoot himself while cleaning the muzzle of his gun with his tongue!

This volume deals with the topic of suicide and not euthanasia. The two terms are often treated synonymously by the media and the public at large. However, suicide involves the preternatural extinction of one's life, as opposed to genuine euthanasia (whether active or passive) that involves the killing or letting die of the terminally ill. Euthanasia—it might be claimed—is an alleged solution for the ills of dying, whereas suicide is an alleged cure for the ills of living.

Obviously, perplexing questions can arise about the exact meaning of expressions like "terminally ill." Full-blown AIDS (Acquired Immune Deficiency Syndrome) always leads to death; but do we want to call an HIV-positive victim who kills himself or is assisted in doing so (in the early stages of the illness) a suicide? What are we to make of the recent case of David Rivlin, a thirty-eight-year-old quadriplegic, who wanted to die because of his condition and his reliance on a respirator? Since he had been judged fully competent, a court order was issued so that his ventilator could be removed. He was given valium and morphine, and then his respirator was turned off. He died some thirty minutes later. Had he not opted for this death, Rivlin might have lived for many more years. Is this assisted suicide, a type of euthanasia, or simply an attempt to gain control over one's own life, the choice of which ultimately ended in death? If we are to put some reasonable restraints on the time factor involved in a terminal illness, it would seem that Rivlin might well have been a suicide.

Unless we are all absurdly declared to be terminally ill simply because every day we are a minute closer to death (existentialists sometimes speak of humans as "beings-unto-death"), it would seem sensible to reserve talk of terminal illness for the time frame of less than a year to live, given the best available medical prognosis about one's physical condition. Accordingly, despite the publicity surrounding his alleged "suicide" in 1981, the death of Nico Speijer, a prominent Dutch suicidologist, was probably more accurately described as a case of voluntary active euthanasia, for Speijer was terminally ill with intestinal cancer that was rapidly metastasizing. The situation of his wife, who died with him, is less obviously a case of euthanasia. By contrast, the suicide pact of Henry Pitney Van Dusen, the former president of Union Theological Seminary, and his wife, Elizabeth, both of whom died from deliberate overdoses of sleeping pills, seems genuine, for while he suffered from the aftereffects of stroke and she from arthritis, neither could reasonably be described as terminally ill (although they were chronically ill).

On the whole, civilized society still frowns upon and shudders at suicide. For example, in 1987, the convicted state treasurer of Pennsylvania committed suicide at a televised press conference, the day before he was to be sentenced to prison for fraud. While the media covered the story, few reputable television stations or newspapers would show the graphic event itself. Yet those same media outlets would not have hesitated to show footage of war scenes, plane crashes, gang shootouts, assassinations, or the latest chainsaw massacre horror film.

What exactly counts as a suicide? Is suicide ever rational or morally justified? Is it ever obligatory? Are suicidal actions—or patterns of self-negligent behavior that result in death—also bona fide suicides? Is it psychiatrically accurate to label successful or unsuccessful suicides as mentally deranged or seriously depressed and, in the case of the unsuccessful, in need of confinement or treatment? Should people who assist or abet others to commit suicide be criminally prosecuted? Is the notion of self-murder an oxymoron? Are all cases of altruistically motivated self-killing really suicides? Are self-annihilations prompted by honor or loyalty—i.e., choosing death over dishonor—genuine suicides? These and a host of related matters will be explored in this volume.

Since the foundations of many contemporary philosophical arguments, either for or against suicide, can be traced back to various important historical thinkers, I thought it appropriate to include two classic essays against suicide (those of Aquinas and Kant), balanced by two classic selections in support of suicide (those of Seneca and Hume).

The historical selections on suicide begin with a pro-suicide essay by Lucius Annaeus Seneca (4 B.C.–A.D. 65), a Roman philosopher and Stoic, who was accused of conspiring to kill Nero, and who subsequently committed suicide upon the emperor's command. Seneca emphasizes considerations of quality of life over mere existence, and recommends dying well as an escape from the ills of living. Human beings have the power and liberty (the right) to exit life when they so choose, and as his gladiator example illustrates, even "the foulest death is preferable to the cleanest slavery." If the vicious can "insult death," all the more appropriate for the virtuous to put a period to their lives. Seneca believed it was criminal to live by robbery, but noble to die by stealing one's own life.

St. Thomas Aquinas (1225–1274) argues against suicide, which he claims is a violation of self-love, love of neighbor or society, and a breach of God's sovereignty over us. Paradoxically, like Seneca, he sees suicide as having features analogous to theft—but the suicide steals God's gift of life, and so misappropriates the property that belongs to God.

Like Seneca, Aquinas prizes human freedom, but the responsible use of it renders no person "judge of himself." Unlike the stoical Seneca, Aquinas fears death and the subsequent judgment of God. Suicide is viewed as a greater sin (moral wrong) than those sins which in time can be repented. Interestingly, Aquinas opposed the martyrdom via suicide of chaste women who were about to be raped; he argues that they need not consent and hence can morally avoid being violated because "evil must not be done that good may come" (or evil be avoided).

David Hume (1711–1776) wholly disagrees with Aquinas, arguing that suicide is not contrary to love of self, of neighbor, or of God. Hume claimed that even assuming the truth of Aquinas' theism, one need not preclude suicide from being rational and moral. That is, if it is religiously permissible to encroach on divine providence by disturbing the operations of various natural laws (by curing diseases and the like), then, by parity of reasoning, it ought to be similarly permissible to commit suicide. Moreover, couldn't a person commit suicide while expressing gratitude to God for the good she has enjoyed and for the ability to escape her current misery? After all, Aquinas allowed self-inflicted killings when one is divinely commanded to do so!

Hume, a known skeptic on religious matters, is being ever so ironical and sardonic in his essay.

> When I fall upon my own sword, therefore I receive my death equally from the hands of the deity as if it had proceeded from a lion, a precipice, or a fever. . . . There is no being which possesses any power or faculty, that it receives not from its Creator; nor is there any one, which by ever so irregular an action, can encroach upon the plan of his providence, or disorder the universe. Its operations are his works equally with that chain of events which it invades; and whichever principle prevails, we may for that very reason conclude it to be most favored by him.

Readers of Hume's *Dialogues Concerning Natural Religion* will be aghast at how his alter-ego, Philo, could ever countenance such thoughts as presented in his essay on suicide. Secular humanists will appreciate Hume's pungent satire, but find themselves taken aback by his bold claim that "the life of a man is of no greater importance to the universe than that of an oyster."

Like Seneca, Hume wants to emphasize our liberty to kill ourselves. It's no more "playing God" to take one's life than it is to preserve one's life. Hume would clearly approve of the suicides of the Van Dusens and David Rivlin. And suicide is not necessarily opposed to the common good. A person is not obligated to do a small good for society at the cost of great harm to himself. Indeed, suicide can even be "laudable" when my continued existence is a burden to society. On March 27, 1984, then Governor of Colorado, Richard Lamm, said: "We've got a duty to die and get out of the way with all of our machines and artificial hearts and everything else like that and let the other society, our kids, build a reasonable life." He went on to say that he would "take the money we could save in reforming the health-care system and put it into . . . restarting America's industrial engine and in the education system."[2] Thus, a person is acting in her own rational self-interest when she prudently and courageously kills herself to avoid the sickness and misfortunes of life.

Defenders of St. Thomas will want to argue that Hume's manoeuvre has overlooked the important distinction between *laws of nature* and *natural laws*. The former are descriptive regulations based on uniform regularities in nature; the latter, the focus of Aquinas' animus toward suicide, are prescriptive rules, ostensibly based on the essential aspects of human nature.

Immanuel Kant (1724–1804), in opposition to both Seneca and Hume, claims that the exercise of freedom in self-destruction is self-contradictory. He seems to favor, however, the moral heroism of Cato (a Roman statesman who committed suicide rather than surrender to Julius Caesar), but does not label it a suicide, since Cato was presumably attempting to rescue his personal integrity and not intending to destroy himself. "If a man cannot preserve his life except by dishonoring his humanity, he ought rather to sacrifice it." Even intemperate, imprudent risk-taking behavior need not be suicide. There are victims of fate who are not suicides.

Despite his anti-suicide stance, Kant claims that there are times when life ought to be sacrificed. "If I cannot preserve my life except by violating my duties towards myself, I am bound to sacrifice my life rather than violate these duties." He views "humanity in one's own person" as "inviolable." Suicide, by contrast, treats our personhood as a thing; it reduces us to the level of a beast. But life is not more important than virtue. "To live is not a necessity; but to live honorably while life lasts is a necessity." Unlike Hume, Kant maintains that the fabric of society is undermined by those who advocate a right to suicide and romanticize it somewhat in the process.

In his critique of suicide, Kant makes some interesting and controversial psychological claims. For example, he avers that a person lacking integrity and self-worth places greater value on biological life, unlike the person of "inner worth" who will sacrifice biological life to retain his or her personhood. In an ingenious thought-experiment, Kant asks us to imagine a group of people, some vicious, some virtuous, all of whom are unjustly accused of a crime and given the choice of death or life imprisonment. He hypothesizes that they would choose as follows: "A man of inner worth does not shrink from death: he would die rather than live as an object of contempt, a member of a gang of scoundrels in the galleys; but the worthless man prefers the galleys, almost as if they were his proper place." Kant is offering the caveat that people shouldn't surrender their personhood to the will of others, and shouldn't preserve their lives at the cost of disgraceful conduct. Kant would appear to approve of the self-killings of hostages held captive in terrorist quarters, as well as the suicide of Judas Iscariot.

From a distinctly religious perspective, Kant sides with Aquinas over Hume in viewing suicide as "abominable." It violates the purpose of creation and is a throwing of the gift in the giver's face, a rebellion against God. "Human beings are sentinels on earth," Kant writes, and "God is our owner, we are His property; His providence works for our good. A bondsman in the care of a beneficent master deserves punishment if he opposes his master's wishes."

R. G. Frey has upset many intellectuals by arguing that Socrates—who was sentenced to death by the Athenian Senate for corrupting the young—knowingly and intentionally drank the hemlock and, accordingly, was a suicide. Frey is not placing moral blame on Socrates for drinking the poison, but only pointing out that not all suicides need be "ignoble and undignified." The context of an Athenian judicial execution need not preclude suicide.[3]

Joseph Fletcher, the famed situation ethicist,* provides a humanist defense of suicide. Whereas Western cultural influences (as well as the Islamic tradition) have opposed suicide, non-Western cultures have long been tolerant of it, as in the Japanese rite of *seppuku* or *hara-kiri*, and the Hindu *suttee*.† St. Augustine probably lent the most authoritative weight against suicide, as he opposed the Donatists who held that dying in a state of grace via suicide was better than living with the risk of lapsing back into sin.

Fletcher contends that "human rights are not self-validating," but, rather, human needs validate rights. Favoring the values of self-determination and liberty, he believes that suicide can often be morally right provided it isn't outweighed by harm to others, for persons are not the mere instruments or property of the church or the state.

In ancient times suicide was a tragic option. It then evolved under the influence of Christianity into a sin. Later it became a crime, and is now often viewed as a sickness. Fletcher prefers to regard suicide as "the signature of freedom," one's last autonomous act.

From historical underpinnings, we shift to a discussion of what counts as suicide. William Tolhurst attempts to shed some light on exactly what constitutes suicide. His article is not an easy read, and some have criticized

---

*No actions are intrinsically right or wrong, but judged according to the context, which determines what maximizes human fulfillment.

†*Seppuku* or *hara-kiri* was the Japanese method of disembowelment with a sword. It was often performed by Samurai warriors who were disgraced, defiant of their superiors, or condemned to death. *Suttee* was the ritual in India's caste system where the widow of a nobleman threw herself upon his funeral pyre and was immolated.

it for yielding much ado about nothing. The notion of suicide is presently very much open-textured,* and cases of apparent suicide are often ambivalent. Agencies reporting mortality rates need to be clear about what constitutes suicide, otherwise their statistical data will be hopelessly skewed (not to mention insurance company death benefits). Insurance policies, religious burial rites, and issues of societal stigma on families and reputations all hinge on greater clarity in defining suicide. Without linguistic precision, we are left with the unsettling relativism inherent in the claim that one person's suicide is another person's heroic act or risk-taking venture. It is far too imprecise to define suicide as just self-inflicted death, and too reflective of societal bias and prejudice to settle the moral issues involved, in advance, by defining suicide as "self-murder."

Tolhurst rejects Emile Durkheim's† classic definition wherein suicide refers to "death resulting directly or indirectly from a positive or negative act of the victim himself, which he knows will produce this result." He also rejects Richard Brandt's proposal, since both accounts make a person's foreknowledge that death will result from one's actions into a sufficient condition of suicide.

Tolhurst continues by rejecting the respective definitions of suicide proposed by Joseph Margolis and Tom Beauchamp, who deny that altruistic motivation or coercion can be compatible with suicide. In rejecting Beauchamp, Tolhurst tries to show how coercion is compatible with suicide as in the case of a person who decides to kill himself by jumping into a ravine, only to encounter on the way an avalanche that kills him.

Tolhurst seeks a definition of suicide that will be both intuitive and plausible. He favors the view that suicide is "successfully implementing a course of action in order to bring about one's death." The reader will have to decide how much in accord with ordinary language Tolhurst's paradigm-cases prove to be. He seems to regard the case of a captured soldier about to be tortured and who, to avoid this, bites and swallows a capsule of cyanide lodged in his dentures, as a clear case of suicide. Granted a choice is involved here, but it is so constrained, it is hard to see how Tolhurst could consider it a *free* choice.

Since the concept of intention enters into almost all definitions of

---

*Many words are linguistically imprecise or indeterminate in meaning. Such terms (e.g., "bald," "tall," "middle-aged," "rich," "poor," etc.) aren't really vague but they are prone to borderline cases.

†Emile Durkheim (1858–1917) was a French sociologist, a pioneer in suicidology, and author of the influential *Suicide: A Study in Sociology* (New York: Free Press, 1951).

suicide, Tolhurst explores a *weak* and *strong* sense of the term "intentional." He claims that for a self-caused death to be suicide it must be strongly intentional. In other words, some act x will be considered strongly intentional if and only if there is an act y that the agent wants to perform and x either generates or is y, and the agent's performance of x is caused in an appropriate way by the agent's desire to do y along with the agent's beliefs about the generation of y. Tolhurst believes that most altruistically motivated, self-caused deaths are not strongly intentional, and hence not suicides.

Tolhurst also takes up the topic that Frey opened: whether Socrates committed suicide. Since Tolhurst believes that an intentional action requires the correct sort of causal history resulting from the person's beliefs and desires, the question comes down to Socrates' act-generating beliefs. Socrates was faced with (a) drinking hemlock, (b) causing his own death, and (c) complying with Athenian law. If we assume that Socrates believed that (a) would generate (b) and (c), and he wanted to do (c), then (a) and (c) do seem strongly intentional, and (b) at least weakly intentional. However, Socrates would not be a suicide if he believed the law required him to drink the hemlock, so that (a) would generate (c) directly, but not that (c) would be generated by (b). However, if Socrates believed that causing his own death was necessary to comply with Athenian law, and that drinking the hemlock would generate that compliance through his death, then Socrates was a suicide.

Tolhurst takes up the complicated matter of deviant causal chains involved in the logic of act-generating beliefs.[4] There can be situations where a person has the appropriate beliefs and desires to kill himself yet doesn't commit suicide, precisely because the actual causal chain does not conform to his action plan. For example, a person wants to commit suicide by jumping from an overhead bridge onto the traffic below, but is fatally shot instead by a stray bullet from an unrelated gang shootout while still standing on the bridge. If this is not to be considered suicide, the causal deviations have to be considerable, to avoid having it fall into that category. An "exact fit" is not required. One cannot avoid suicide by wanting to shoot oneself in the head, but out of nervousness, shoot oneself instead in the heart. However, until the matter of deviant causal chains is resolved, Tolhurst believes we cannot definitively "say whether particular self-caused deaths which result from causal chains which do not exactly coincide with the agent's action-plan are suicides or not."

Some suggest that Socrates was not the only historically significant suicide; Jesus may well have been one also. More recently, questions have been raised about the death in 1981 of the Irish Republican Army provisional Bobby Sands, who died in Northern Ireland while on a well-publicized hunger strike. Were any of these persons suicides? Suzanne Stern-Gillet thinks that none of them were. She views their deaths as induced, and suggests that how one decides the matter of responsibility-ascription here is very often politically motivated. She reminds us that inherent in the descriptive meaning of suicide is a normative component—the ascription of moral responsibility—that is "inextricably intermingled" with the descriptive meaning. In short, in making decisions on whether a particular self-engineered death was a suicide, one is also making a value judgment.

Stern-Gillet, unlike Tolhurst, seems to think that a definition, or an assessment, of suicide cannot be conclusively settled in any empirical way. Stressing the inherent responsibility-ascription in suicide assessment, there are bound to be intractable disputes over whether Socrates or Bobby Sands committed suicide. Some will argue that in such cases the victims brought on their own deaths; others will say instead that the Athenian or British government bears responsibility for these killings. Given such normative disputes, moral praise or blame will vary accordingly, and the issue of suicide or martyrdom will turn on how one views the responsibility-ascribing function.

R. G. Frey challenges the widely accepted belief that suicide must be self-inflicted. He contends that there are cases where a person wants to die (either as an end or a means), and so knowingly and willingly places himself in a perilous situation that results in death. The polar explorer Captain Oates would seem to be a suicide, although his death is other-inflicted by the Antarctic blizzard. The verdict of suicide may also be arguably assigned to a father who dies after sacrificing his only remaining kidney to save the life of his young son.

Frey develops some interesting scenarios to show how suicide can be other-inflicted (e.g., the actor who puts real bullets in a gun that he knows will be fired at him in a play; the unhappy person who challenges a superior gunman to a duel; and the despondent husband who taunts and humiliates his wife incessantly in order to manipulate her into killing him in a fit of passion). Of course, if the other party involved really wanted to kill the suicide victim, then we have a case of both murder and suicide.

Frey is making the important point that just because death is other-inflicted doesn't mean that the victim isn't a suicide, provided the suicide wanted and contrived the death by exploiting and manipulating the other party to do it. It should come as no surprise that a number of suicides are disguised in this manner.

Terence O'Keeffe focuses on the religious prohibition of suicide, especially the "life as a gift" thesis and its corollary, the divine ownership theory, as elucidated by such philosophers as Augustine, Aquinas, Locke, and Kant. From this religious perspective, suicide has also been condemned by such modern writers as Gilbert Chesterton, who compared suicide to omnicide (the killing of everything), and Ludwig Wittgenstein, who called suicide "the elementary sin."

O'Keeffe also considers cases of heroic self-sacrifice such as Maximilian Kolbe and Captain Oates. He thinks they are not suicides since there was no overriding intent to die. They are cases of instrumental self-killings where the act is performed for some paramount altruistic and overriding purpose. To be genuine suicides persons must intend to kill themselves, and there must be no other primary, independent objective involved in the action. In short, the self-engineered death must be noninstrumental.

Like many philosophers, O'Keeffe takes up the principle of double effect, but he interprets it as being primarily about acts and their effects, and not about intentions as such. He defines the principle of double effect as follows: "(1) the action must itself be a good action or at least morally neutral; (2) the performance of the action must bring about at least as much good as evil; (3) the evil effect must not be a means to achieving the good effect; and (4) the agent must have a justifying and sufficient reason for acting rather than refraining from acting." He seems to suggest that some cases of heroic, altruistic self-killing would escape the potentially harsh verdict of suicide by use of the principle of double effect.[5]

O'Keeffe offers an interesting thought-experiment, a sort of post-mortem verification test, to determine if a person's death was really a suicide. He asks us to imagine that these suicides are momentarily revived. Genuine suicides (i.e., noninstrumental self-killers) would be distressed and want to die again. But instrumental self-killers would take delight in being revived, and only be tempted to redo their deaths if the paramount causes for which their lives were offered remained unaccomplished.

O'Keeffe admits that on his account the religious sin of suicide is "an almost inconceivable act." This is so because in order to be a genuine suicide, one must kill oneself from a sheer hatred of self, of world, of life, or of God. Suicide, for O'Keeffe, is the ultimate nihilistic act. His account does not justify all instrumental self-killings, for the cause served must itself be noble and worthy. He believes the hunger strikes in Northern Ireland during the early 1980s were not justifiable; he seems to suggest that Bobby Sands, and those of like mind, were not genuine suicides, however imprudent their actions may have been.

Glenn Graber defines suicide as "doing something that results in one's death in the way that was planned, either from the intention of ending one's life or the intention to bring about some other state of affairs (such as relief from pain) that one thinks it certain or highly probable can be achieved only by means of death." The intention in question must be *strong,* as specified in the earlier analysis of Tolhurst. Interestingly, Graber would not label as genuine suicides cases in which an agent attempts suicide as a desperate plea for help rather than a desire to die, but who nonetheless does die as a result. Persons could hang themselves or take an overdose of sleeping pills and still not be properly classified as suicides, for they lacked the strong intention to die.

Graber, like Brandt, believes that suicide can sometimes be rational when "a reasonable appraisal of the situation reveals that one is really better off dead," that is, "the value of the benefits of which immediate death would rob them is outweighed by the disvalue of the pain from which death would spare them." On the whole, Graber, like Seneca, grants final authority regarding the rationality of suicide to the first-person judgment of the individual contemplating suicide, provided that the person is factually and conceptually clear about the situation and is not so nihilistic as to see no value in life or any disvalue in death.

Edwin Shneidman, the famed suicidologist, begins the discussion in Part Three on the rationality and morality of suicide. He is convinced that suicide is wrong, and urges us to identify and treat various would-be suicides. He compares suicide prevention techniques to those of fire prevention, and cautions us to be on the lookout for various "clues" that indicate a likely suicide attempt. He assumes that those who attempt suicide are really ambivalent about their wishes and at heart want to be rescued. Paternalistic intervention to salvage potential suicides is not a source of concern: "only by being free to see the possibility of suicide potential in everybody can suicide prevention of anybody really become effective." We must err on the side of vigilance. The reader must decide if Shneidman's paternalism is warranted, especially in light of the various suicidal symptoms he identifies in numerous verbal, behavioral, and situational contexts.

Thomas Szasz, a psychiatrist, regards the attitude of suicidologists like

Shneidman as both "erroneous" and "evil." The anti-suicide posture is erroneous because it views any suicide as an event and not an action, and evil because it legitimizes force and fraud in suicide prevention under the guise of medical treatment. "Suicide is medical heresy. Commitment and electroshock are the appropriate psychiatric-inquisitorial remedies for it."

Szasz claims that the suicidal person is not necessarily mentally ill. Ever-vigilant suicidologists mistakenly treat a desire to die and to exercise autonomy over one's death as if it were a disease. Physicians do not involuntarily hospitalize patients who refuse to take their life-sustaining medications, yet they think nothing of intervening with potential suicides and incarcerating them if need be.

Szasz, like Seneca and Fletcher, holds the libertarian notion that the individual has a right to commit suicide (his or her person neither belongs to the state nor is owned by God). Just as there is no self-theft, so there is no self-murder (assuming that our lives belong to us) where alleged criminal and victim are the same person. Szasz grants that some medical interventions without the patient's consent are warranted, as when treating a fractured limb or in other purely mechanical acts on the body. But suicide prevention is more a political act than a medical one, depriving persons of their liberty, and dehumanizing them in the process. The suicidologist reacts with involuntary confinement, electroshock, lobotomy, and slavery. Szasz offers a striking comparison of the way the medical community treats a potential suicide and how various totalitarian governments treat would-be emigrés.

The essay by Milton Gonsalves is a classic statement of the theistic position against suicide, which is defined as the "direct killing of oneself on one's own authority," wherein "death is intended either as an end or as a means to an end." Reminiscent of the methodological style of Aquinas, Gonsalves begins by considering six plausible and persuasive arguments for suicide, and attempts to respond to each. To those who claim that it is rational to kill oneself when life becomes so burdensome that the individual is useless to himself and to society, Gonsalves responds by emphasizing how suffering can be redemptive and character-building. To those who stress the right to commit suicide as a last dignified act of self-mastery, Gonsalves counters that it violates our duty to love ourselves and to preserve our existence. The third argument underscores that death can be the lesser of two evils; but for Gonsalves it is wrong to choose the lesser of two physical evils when moral evil is involved.

The fourth pro-suicide argument claims that God's gift of life is unrestricted, and so can be relinquished when to continue it is more harmful than beneficial. Gonsalves responds by claiming that God's gift is restricted, and we are meant to be stewards over life, not lords and masters. To the fifth argument, Gonsalves responds that while an omniscient God cannot be defrauded by those who return the gift of life via suicide, it is wrong to seek to defraud God. The sixth argument emphasizes the allowing of killing in self-defense as well as the state's legal killings in war and capital punishment; but Gonsalves retorts by pointing out that the suicide is both attacker and the attacked, executioner and murderer, so the analogies drawn with self-defense and state executions are not appropriate.

Richard Brandt believes persons may have a *prima facie* rather than an absolute obligation not to commit suicide. He reminds us that even if a particular suicide is morally wrong, it may nonetheless be excusable (if, for example, the suicide acted out of a sense of duty or was in an unsound state of mind). Brandt finds fault with the arguments of Aquinas, Locke, and Kant who reject suicide, especially via the divine ownership argument.

Brandt, a utilitarian, contends that suicide involves a "choice between future world-courses." Those contemplating suicide must use the very best empirical information available about their situation, and take all their desires into account. Agents' future desires and preferences are to count as much as their present ones. The decision to kill oneself should never be made in a state of depression, which tends "to primitivize one's intellectual processes," repressing one's memory of countervailing evidence, and affecting one's judgment about probable future events. However, if it becomes clear beyond a reasonable doubt that future existence is not preferable to eliminating one's present misery, it is rational for the agents to kill themselves, i.e., to choose a world-course that contains their early demise. In short, Brandt, like Graber, defends the notion of balance-sheet suicide (*Bilanzselbstmord*).

Brandt also offers some reflections on the role of an advisor to the potential suicide. He thinks it is appropriate at times for paternalistic intervention to stop the suicide. However, on other occasions, it may be appropriate to help a person commit suicide, provided it doesn't involve any great cost to the advisor.

In contrast to Brandt, Philip Devine argues that it is not rational to choose death via egocentric suicide (given the assumption that there is no life after death), because one can have no knowledge about the choice to die, either through self-experience or through the testimony of others.

In short, death manifests a "logical opaqueness," so that the option for death is not a genuine alternative. Rational choice between life and death requires considerable knowledge about both options, and since death is unknowable, suicide involves pathetic risk taking. Quite obviously, there is no opportunity, once suicide is committed, to check one's losses. So, Devine rejects Brandt's limited defense of the morality and rationality of suicide because the world-course of death cannot be experienced. Devine reminds us that there is a big difference between a painless existence that (while alive) we prefer versus freedom from pain when we are nonexistent. (The reader might ask whether, given Devine's thesis about death's opaqueness, the choice *not* to commit suicide can, by contrast, be rational.)

Joyce Carol Oates would disagree with Seneca, Hume, Graber, Brandt, Fletcher, and Szasz. She regards as foolish, if not immoral, most suicides of an egocentric sort. She faults the literary and philosophical tradition for romanticizing suicide, and viewing it as the quintessentially free, rational, and creative act. The fundamental error of justifications offered for suicide is an aesthetic one, because the victim is misled by metaphors. Death is not liberating, but a mere brute inarticulateness. It is sheer, unwarranted romanticism to describe death as the last journey, everlasting sleep, perpetual rest, eternal peace, the absence of life, or the Jungian "profound peace of all-knowing non-existence." The suicide as artist is rightly labeled neurotic or deranged. If there is no life after death, then death cannot be rationally chosen, because it remains unexperienced and unimaginable.

Søren Kierkegaard, reflecting on death in his *Concluding Unscientific Postscript*—albeit not on suicide per se—writes about students taking an exam that they have four hours to complete. The students have the option of taking the whole four hours allotted. The *task* of finishing the exam is one matter; time itself is another. However, when time itself is the very assignment, i.e., the task of life, then it is wrong to finish before the time has transpired. That is, if life constitutes the task, then "to be finished with life before life has finished with one, is precisely not to have finished the task."[6]

Is suicide right? Is it wrong? Is it noble? Is it ignoble? Each reader must grapple for an answer to these and a host of other queries raised in the essays and selections that follow. It is my personal hope that no reader will find it necessary to opt for suicide.[7] But if reason fails to convince, then perhaps we can all find some ironic distance to appreciate the sardonic ditty of Dorothy Parker, who advised:

Razors pain you;
Rivers are damp;
Acids stain you;
And drugs cause cramp;
Guns aren't lawful;
Nooses give;
Gas smells awful;
You might as well live.[8]

NOTES

1. Baffling questions surface for suicidologists as to why in these high-risk groups, some people do commit or attempt suicide while others do not. Among other perplexing issues, one wonders why there is a high rate of suicide in such Scandinavian countries as Finland, Sweden, and Denmark, but a much lower rate in Norway. Do media coverage and school instructional programs about suicide actually generate a greater propensity for suicidal behavior, as in the phenomenon of "copy-cat" suicides?

2. *U.S. News and World Report* (April 9, 1984): 18.

3. Michael Smith, unlike Frey, argues that it is false that anyone who knowingly, say, smokes or drinks while aware of the health hazards involved, thereby wants to be sick. It might be granted that Socrates drank the hemlock intentionally and presumably desired to do so either as an end in itself or as a means to some end, but "it does not follow that Socrates wants to die just because he knows that drinking the hemlock is a means to that end and drinks the hemlock intentionally" ("Did Socrates Kill Himself Intentionally?" *Philosophy* 55 [1980]: 253–54).

Harry Lesser points out that to define suicide as "killing oneself intentionally," and treating suicide as somehow synonymous with "self-murder," is unfortunate. The latter description makes any suicide wrong by definition since it involves killing oneself unlawfully and maliciously. But Socrates' "suicide" was neither illegal nor performed maliciously. Lesser claims that Socrates' "suicide" was intentional, since he cooperated in his own execution, though he was acting under moral duress ("Suicide and Self-Murder," *Philosophy* 55 [1980]: 255–57).

4. Like Tolhurst, Michael Wreen (in "The Definition of Suicide," *Social Theory and Practice* 14 [1988]: 1–23) deals with the logic of deviant causal chains and intentions. In general, Wreen thinks that most cases of heroic self-sacrifice are similar to typical refusal-of-treatment cases that result in death, and so should not be regarded as suicide. According to Wreen, a person commits suicide at time t if and only if: (1) the person strongly intends to kill himself (or strongly wants to let himself die) at t; (2) the person killed himself at t; (3) the intention

in (1) caused (2) via the intermediary of a number of generated actions; (4) the causal route from (1) to (2) was more or less in accord with his action plan; and (5) the person acted voluntarily in killing himself.

5. O'Keeffe's formulation of the principle of double effect differs from many other such formulations, especially with respect to the second condition. Often that second condition states that the agent's intention is not directly to do the evil that results since it is only foreseen. No matter how it is formulated, the principle (representing the epitome of casuistry) is designed to offset the consequential harm often involved in dutiful adherence to a moral rule. Some ethicists have believed the principle could be used to at least condone suicide.

6. (Princeton: Princeton University Press, 1968), p. 147. Like the Stoics, Kierkegaard thinks it is mistaken to speak of suicide as a cowardly act. In fact, he suspects cowardice often masquerades as courage in motivating people to refrain from suicide. And, while Kierkegaard's anti-suicide stance is largely motivated by religious considerations (suicide is viewed as a "rebellion" against God), he is rather novel in treating suicide as a "jailbreak" from the prison of existence. Unlike many religious philosophers, Kierkegaard doesn't view suicide as ingratitude against God. To think so is "a lie and rubbish, the swindle which the prison has invented for mutual support in the notion that it is a splendid world" (*Journals and Papers*, #4733). Rather, eternal salvation awaits those who patiently endure their respective pre-mortem, suffering lives.

7. Anyone who may be interested in my own position and arguments against suicide might read *Language, Metaphysics, and Death* (New York: Fordham University Press, 1978), pp. 88-105.

8. John Morreall, *Taking Laughter Seriously* (Albany: State University of New York Press, 1983), p. 129.

Part One
Some Historical Background

1

The Stoic View

Seneca

. . . Life has carried some men with the greatest rapidity to the harbor, the harbor they were bound to reach even if they tarried on the way, while others it has fretted and harassed. To such a life, as you are aware, one should not always cling. For mere living is not a good, but living well. Accordingly, the wise man will live as long as he ought, not as long as he can. He will mark in what place, with whom, and how he is to conduct his existence, and what he is about to do. He always reflects concerning the quality, and not the quantity, of his life. As soon as there are many events in his life that give him trouble and disturb his peace of mind, he sets himself free. And this privilege is his, not only when the crisis is upon him, but as soon as Fortune seems to be playing him false; then he looks about carefully and sees whether he ought, or ought not, to end his life on that account. He holds that it makes no difference to him whether his taking-off be natural or self-inflicted, whether it comes later or earlier. He does not regard it with fear, as if it were a great loss; for no man can lose very much when but a driblet remains. It is not

"On the Proper Time to Slip the Cable," reprinted by permission of the publishers and the Loeb Classical Library from Seneca, *Epistulae Morales,* Vol. II, R. M. Gummere, trans. (Cambridge, Mass.: Harvard University Press, 1920).

a question of dying earlier or later, but of dying well or ill. And dying well means escape from the danger of living ill.

That is why I regard the words of the well-known Rhodian[1] as most unmanly. This person was thrown into a cage by his tyrant, and fed there like some wild animal. And when a certain man advised him to end his life by fasting, he replied: "A man may hope for anything while he has life." This may be true; but life is not to be purchased at any price. No matter how great or how well-assured certain rewards may be, I shall not strive to attain them at the price of a shameful confession of weakness. Shall I reflect that Fortune has all power over one who lives, rather than reflect that she has no power over one who knows how to die? There are times, nevertheless, when a man, even though certain death impends and he knows that torture is in store for him, will refrain from lending a hand to his own punishment; to himself, however, he would lend a hand.[2] It is folly to die through fear of dying. The executioner is upon you; wait for him. Why anticipate him? Why assume the management of a cruel task that belongs to another? Do you grudge your executioner his privilege, or do you merely relieve him of his task? Socrates might have ended his life by fasting; he might have died by starvation rather than by poison. But instead of this he spent thirty days in prison awaiting death, not with the idea "everything may happen," or "so long an interval has room for many a hope" but in order that he might show himself submissive to the laws and make the last moments of Socrates an edification to his friends. What would have been more foolish than, scorning death, at the same time to be afraid of poison?

Scribonia, a woman of the stern old type, was an aunt of Drusus Libo.[3] This young man was as stupid as he was well born, with higher ambitions than anyone could have been expected to entertain in that epoch, or a man like himself in any epoch at all. When Libo had been carried away ill from the senate-house in his litter, though certainly with a very scanty train of followers—for all his kinsfolk undutifully deserted him, when he was no longer a criminal but a corpse,—he began to consider whether he should commit suicide, or await death. Scribonia said to him: "What pleasure do you find in doing another man's work?" But he did not follow her advice; he laid violent hands upon himself. And he was right, after all; for when a man is doomed to die in two or three days at his enemy's pleasure, he is really "doing another man's work" if he continues to live.

No general statement can be made, therefore, with regard to the question whether, when a power beyond our control threatens us with death, we should anticipate death, or await it. For there are more arguments to pull us in either direction. If one death is accompanied by torture, and the other is simple and easy, why not snatch the latter? Just as I shall select my ship when I am about to go on a voyage, or my house when I propose to take a residence, so I shall choose my death when I am about to depart from life. Moreover, just as a long-drawn-out life does not necessarily mean a better one, so a long-drawn-out death necessarily means a worse one. There is no occasion when the soul should be humored more than at the moment of death. Let the soul depart as it feels itself impelled to go,[4] whether it seeks the sword, or the halter, or some draught that attacks the veins, let it proceed and burst the bonds of its slavery. Every man ought to make his life acceptable to others besides himself, but his death to himself alone. The best form of death is the one we like. Men are foolish who reflect thus: "One person will say that my conduct was not brave enough; another, that I was too headstrong; a third, that a particular kind of death would have betokened more spirit." What you should really reflect is: "I have under consideration a purpose with which the talk of men has no concern!" Your sole aim should be to escape from Fortune as speedily as possible; otherwise, there will be no lack of persons who will think ill of what you have done.

You can find men who have gone so far as to profess wisdom and yet maintain that one should not offer violence to one's own life, and hold it accursed for a man to be the means of his own destruction; we should wait, say they, for the end decreed by nature. But one who says this does not see that he is shutting off the path to freedom. The best thing which eternal law ever ordained was that it allowed to us one entrance into life, but many exits. Must I await the cruelty either of disease or of man, when I can depart through the midst of torture, and shake off my troubles? This is the one reason why we cannot complain of life: it keeps no one against his will. Humanity is well situated, because no man is unhappy except by his own fault. Live, if you so desire; if not, you may return to the place whence you came. You have often been cupped in order to relieve headaches. You have had veins cut for the purpose of reducing your weight. If you would pierce your heart, a gaping wound is not necessary; a lancet will open the way to that great freedom, and tranquillity can be purchased at the cost of a pin-prick.

What, then, is it which makes us lazy and sluggish? None of us reflects that some day he must depart from this house of life; just so old tenants are kept from moving by fondness for a particular place and by custom, even in spite of ill-treatment. Would you be free from the restraint of your body? Live in it as if you were about to leave it. Keep thinking of the fact that some day you will be deprived of this tenure; then you will be more brave against the necessity of departing. But how will a man take thought of his own end, if he craves all things without end? And yet there is nothing so essential for us to consider. For our training in other things is perhaps superfluous. Our souls have been made ready to meet poverty; but our riches have held out. We have armed ourselves to scorn pain; but we have had the good fortune to possess sound and healthy bodies, and so have never been forced to put this virtue to the test. We have taught ourselves to endure bravely the loss of those we love; but Fortune has preserved to us all whom we loved. It is in this one matter only that the day will come which will require us to test our training.

You need not think that none but great men have had the strength to burst the bonds of human servitude; you need not believe that this cannot be done except by a Cato,—Cato, who with his hand dragged forth the spirit which he had not succeeded in freeing by the sword. Nay, men of the meanest lot in life have by a mighty impulse escaped to safety, and when they were not allowed to die at their own convenience, or to suit themselves in their choice of the instruments of death, they have snatched up whatever was lying ready to hand, and by sheer strength have turned objects which were by nature harmless into weapons of their own. For example, there was lately in a training-school for wild-beast gladiators a German, who was making ready for the morning exhibition; he withdrew in order to relieve himself,—the only thing which he was allowed to do in secret and without the presence of a guard. While so engaged, he seized the stick of wood, tipped with a sponge, which was devoted to the vilest uses, and stuffed it, just as it was, down his throat; thus he blocked up his windpipe, and choked the breath from his body. That was truly to insult death! Yes, indeed; it was not a very elegant or becoming way to die; but what is more foolish than to be over-nice about dying? What a brave fellow! He surely deserved to be allowed to choose his fate! How bravely he would have wielded a sword! With what courage he would have hurled himself into the depths of the sea, or down a precipice! Cut off from resources on every hand, he yet found a way to furnish himself with death, and with a weapon for death. Hence you can understand that nothing but the will need postpone death. Let each man judge the deed of this most zealous fellow as he likes, provided we agree on this point,—that the foulest death is preferable to the cleanest slavery.

Inasmuch as I began with an illustration taken from humble life, I shall keep on with that sort. For men will make greater demands upon themselves, if they see that death can be despised even by the most despised class of men. The Catos, the Scipios, and the others whose names we are wont to hear with admiration, we regard as beyond the sphere of imitation; but I shall now prove to you that the virtue of which I speak is found as frequently in the gladiators' training-school, as among the leaders in a civil war. Lately, a gladiator, who had been sent forth to the morning exhibition, was being conveyed in a cart along with the other prisoners; nodding as if he were heavy with sleep, he let his head fall over so far that it was caught in the spokes; then he kept his body in position long enough to break his neck by the revolution of the wheel. So he made his escape by means of the very wagon which was carrying him to his punishment.

When a man desires to burst forth and take his departure, nothing stands in his way. It is an open space in which Nature guards us. When our plight is such as to permit it, we may look about us for an easy exit. If you have many opportunities ready to hand, by means of which you may liberate yourself, you may make a selection and think over the best way of gaining freedom; but if a chance is hard to find, instead of the best, snatch the next best, even though it be something unheard of, something new. If you do not lack the courage, you will not lack the cleverness to die. See how even the lowest class of slave, when suffering goads him on, is aroused and discovers a way to deceive even the most watchful guards! He is truly great who not only has given himself the order to die, but has also found the means.

I have promised you, however, some more illustrations drawn from the same games. During the second event in a sham sea-fight one of the barbarians sank deep into his own throat a spear which had been given him for use against his foe. "Why, oh why," he said, "have I not long ago escaped from all this torture and all this mockery? Why should I be armed and yet wait for death to come?" This exhibition was all the more striking because of the lesson men learn from it that dying is more honorable than killing.

What, then? If such a spirit is possessed by abandoned and dangerous men, shall it not be possessed also by those who have trained themselves to meet such contingencies by long meditation, and by reason, the mistress of all things? It is reason which teaches us that fate has various ways of approach, but the same end, and that it makes no difference at what point the inevitable event begins. Reason, too, advises us to die, if we may, according to our taste; if this cannot be, she advises us to die according to our ability, and to seize upon whatever means shall offer itself for doing violence to ourselves. It is criminal to "live by robbery"; but, on the other hand, it is most noble to "die by robbery." Farewell.

NOTES

1. Telesphorus of Rhodes, threatened by the tyrant Lysimachus.

2. *I.e.,* if he must choose between helping along his punishment by suicide, or helping himself by staying alive under torture and practicing the virtues thus brought into play, he will choose the latter,—*sibi commodare.*

3. For a more complete account of this tragedy see Tacitus, *Annals,* ii. 27 ff. Libo was duped by Firmius Catus (A.D. 16) into seeking imperial power, was detected, and finally forced by Tiberius to commit suicide.

4. When the "natural advantages" of living are outweighed by the corresponding disadvantages, the honorable man may, according to the general Stoic view, take his departure. Socrates and Cato were right in so doing, according to Seneca; but he condemns (*Ep.* xxiv. 25) those contemporaries who had recourse to suicide as a mere whim of fashion.

2

The Catholic View

St. Thomas Aquinas

We proceed thus to the Fifth Article:

Objection 1. It would seem lawful for a man to kill himself. For murder is a sin insofar as it is contrary to justice. But no man can do an injustice to himself, as is proved in *Ethic.* v. 11.[1] Therefore no man sins by killing himself.

Obj. 2. Further, It is lawful, for one who exercises public authority, to kill evildoers. Now he who exercises public authority is sometimes an evildoer. Therefore he may lawfully kill himself.

Obj. 3. Further, It is lawful for a man to suffer spontaneously a lesser danger that he may avoid a greater: Thus it is lawful for a man to cut off a decayed limb even from himself, that he may save his whole body. Now sometimes a man, by killing himself, avoids a greater evil, for an example an unhappy life, or the shame of sin. Therefore a man may kill himself.

Obj. 4. Further, Samson killed himself, as related in Judges xvi, and

---

From volume 2 of Thomas Aquinas, "Whether It Is Lawful to Kill Oneself?" *Summa Theologica* (New York: Benziger Brothers, Inc.; London: Burns & Oaks, Ltd., 1925), Part 2, Question 64, A5. Reprinted by permission of the publishers.

yet he is numbered among the saints (Heb. xi). Therefore it is lawful for a man to kill himself.

Obj. 5. Further, It is related (2 Mach. xiv. 42) that a certain Razias killed himself, *choosing to die nobly rather than to fall into the hands of the wicked, and to suffer abuses unbecoming his noble birth.* Now nothing that is done nobly and bravely is unlawful. Therefore suicide is not unlawful.

On the contrary, Augustine says (*De Civ. Dei i.* 20): *Hence it follows that the words "Thou shalt not kill" refer to the killing of a man; not another man; therefore, not even thyself. For he who kills himself, kills nothing else than a man.*

I answer that, It is altogether unlawful to kill oneself, for three reasons. First, because everything naturally loves itself, the result being that everything naturally keeps itself in being, and resists corruption as far as it can. Wherefore suicide is contrary to the inclination of nature, and to charity whereby every man should love himself. Hence suicide is always a mortal sin, as being contrary to the natural law and to charity.

Secondly, because every part, as such, belongs to the whole. Now every man is part of the community, and so, as such, he belongs to the community. Hence by killing himself he injures the community, as the Philosopher declares (*Ethic.* v. ii).

Thirdly, because life is God's gift to man, and is subject to His power, Who kills and makes to live. Hence whoever takes his own life, sins against God, even as he who kills another's slave, sins against that slave's master, and as he who usurps himself judgment of a matter not entrusted to him. For it belongs to God alone to pronounce sentence of death and life, according to Deut. xxxii. 39, *I will kill and I will make to live.*

Reply Obj. 1. Murder is a sin, not only because it is contrary to justice, but also because it is opposed to charity which a man should have towards himself: in this respect suicide is a sin in relation to oneself. In relation to the community and to God, it is sinful, by reason also of its opposition to justice.

Reply Obj. 2. One who exercises public authority may lawfully put to death an evildoer, since he can pass judgment on him. But no man is judge of himself. Wherefore it is not lawful for one who exercises public authority to put himself to death for any sin whatever: although he may lawfully commit himself to the judgment of others.

Reply Obj. 3. Man is made master of himself through his free-will: wherefore he can lawfully dispose of himself as to those matters which pertain to this life which is ruled by man's free-will. But the passage from this life to another and happier one is subject not to man's free-will but to the power of God. Hence it is not lawful for man to take his own life that he may pass to a happier life, nor that he may escape any unhappiness whatsoever of the present life, because the ultimate and most fearsome evil of this life is death, as the Philosopher states (*Ethic.* iii. 6). Therefore to bring death upon oneself in order to escape the other afflictions of this life, is to adopt a greater evil in order to avoid a lesser. In like manner it is unlawful to take one's own life on account of one's having committed a sin, both because by so doing one does oneself a very great injury, by depriving oneself of the time needful for repentance, and because it is not lawful to slay an evildoer except by the sentence of the public authority. Again it is unlawful for a woman to kill herself lest she be violated, because she ought not to commit on herself the very great sin of suicide, to avoid the lesser sin of another. For she commits no sin in being violated by force, provided she does not consent, since *without consent of the mind there is no stain on the body,* as the Blessed Lucy declared. Now it is evident that fornication and adultery are less grievous sins than taking a man's, especially one's own, life; since the latter is most grievous, because one injures oneself, to whom one owes the greatest love. Moreover it is most dangerous since no time is left wherein to expiate it by repentance. Again it is not lawful for anyone to take his own life for fear he should consent to sin, because *evil must not be done that good may come* (Rom. iii. 8) or that evil may be avoided, especially if the evil be of small account and an uncertain event, for it is uncertain whether one will at some future time consent to a sin, since God is able to deliver man from sin under any temptation whatever.

Reply Obj. 4. As Augustine says (*De Civ. Dei* i. 21), *not even Samson is to be excused that he crushed himself together with his enemies under the ruins of the house, except the Holy Ghost, Who had wrought many wonders through him, had secretly commanded him to do this.* He assigns the same reason in the case of certain holy women, who at the time of persecution took their own lives, and who are commemorated by the Church.

Reply Obj. 5. It belongs to fortitude that a man does not shrink from being slain by another, for the sake of the good of virtue, and that he may avoid sin. But that a man take his own life in order to avoid penal evils has indeed an appearance of fortitude (for which reasons some, among whom was Razias, have killed themselves, thinking to act from fortitude), yet it is not true fortitude, but rather a weakness of soul unable to bear penal evils, as the Philosopher (*Ethic.* iii. 7) and Augustine (*De Civ. Dei* i. 22, 23) declare.

NOTE

1. The reference is to Aristotle's *Nicomachean Ethics*.

3

Reason and Superstition

David Hume

One considerable advantage that arises from philosophy, consists in the sovereign antidote which it affords to superstition and false religion. All other remedies against that pestilent distemper are vain, or at least uncertain. Plain good sense, and the practice of the world, which alone serve most purposes of life, are here found ineffectual: history, as well as daily experience, furnish instances of men endowed with the strongest capacity for business and affairs, who have all their lives crouched under slavery to the grossest superstition. Even gaiety and sweetness of temper, which infuse a balm into every other wound, afford no remedy to so virulent a poison, as we may particularly observe of the fair sex, who, though commonly possessed of these rich presents of nature, feel many of their joys blasted by this importunate intruder. But when sound philosophy has once gained possession of the mind, superstition is effectually excluded; and one may fairly affirm, that her triumph over this enemy is more complete than over most of the vices and imperfections incident to human nature. Love or anger, ambition or avarice, have their root in the temper and affections, which the soundest reason is scarce

Reprinted from David Hume, "On Suicide," *The Philosophical Works of David Hume* (London: Adam and Charles Black, 1826).

ever able fully to correct; but superstition being founded on false opinion, must immediately vanish when true philosophy has inspired juster sentiments of superior powers. The contest is here more equal between the distemper and the medicine; and nothing can hinder the latter from proving effectual, but its being false and sophisticated.

It will here be superfluous to magnify the merits of Philosophy by displaying the pernicious tendency of that vice of which it cures the human mind. The superstitious man, says Tully,[1] is miserable in every scene, in every incident in life; even sleep itself, which banishes all other cares of unhappy mortals, affords to him matter of new terror, while he examines his dreams, and finds in those visions of the night prognostications of future calamities. I may add, that though death alone can put a full period to his misery, he dares not fly to this refuge, but still prolongs a miserable existence, from a vain fear lest he offend his Maker, by using the power with which that beneficent being has endowed him. The presents of God and nature are ravished from us by this cruel enemy; and notwithstanding that one step would remove us from the regions of pain and sorrow, her menaces still chain us down to a hated being, which she herself chiefly contributes to render miserable.

It is observed by such as have been reduced by the calamities of life to the necessity of employing this fatal remedy, that if the unseasonable care of their friends deprive them of that species of death which they proposed to themselves, they seldom venture upon any other, or can summon up so much resolution a second time, as to execute their purpose. So great is our horror of death, that when it presents itself under any form besides that to which a man has endeavored to reconcile his imagination, it acquires new terrors, and overcomes his feeble courage; but when the menaces of superstition are joined to this natural timidity, no wonder it quite deprives men of all power over their lives, since even many pleasures and enjoyments, to which we are carried by a strong propensity, are torn from us by this inhuman tyrant. Let us here endeavor to restore men to their native liberty, by examining all the common arguments against suicide, and showing that that action may be free from every imputation of guilt or blame, according to the sentiments of all the ancient philosophers.

If suicide be criminal, it must be a transgression of our duty either to God, our neighbor, or ourselves. To prove that suicide is no transgression of our duty to God, the following considerations may perhaps suffice. In order to govern the material world, the almighty Creator has established general and immutable laws, by which all bodies, from the greatest planet to the smallest particle of matter, are maintained in their proper sphere and function. To govern the animal world, he has endowed all living creatures with bodily and mental powers; with senses, passions, appetites, memory, and judgment, by which they are impelled or regulated in that course of life to which they are destined. These two distinct principles of the material and animal world continually encroach upon each other, and mutually retard or forward each other's operation. The powers of men and of all other animals are restrained and directed by the nature and qualities of the surrounding bodies; and the modifications and actions of these bodies are incessantly altered by the operation of all animals. Man is stopped by rivers in his passage over the surface of the earth; and rivers, when properly directed, lend their force to the motions of machines, which serve to the use of man. But though the provinces of the material and animal powers are not kept entirely separate, there results from thence no discord or disorder in the creation; on the contrary, from the mixture, union, and contrast of all the various powers of inanimate bodies and living creatures, arises that sympathy, harmony, and proportion, which affords the surest argument of Supreme Wisdom. The providence of the Deity appears not immediately in any operation, but governs every thing by those general and immutable laws which have been established from the beginning of time. All events, in one sense, may be pronounced the action of the Almighty; they all proceed from those powers with which he has endowed his creatures. A house which falls by its own weight, is not brought to ruin by his providence, more than one destroyed by the hands of men; nor are the human faculties less his workmanship than the laws of motion and gravitation. When the passions play, when the judgment dictates, when the limbs obey; this is all the operation of God; and upon these animate principles, as well as upon the inanimate, has he established the government of the universe. Every event is alike important in the eyes of that infinite Being, who takes in at one glance the most distant regions of space, and remotest periods of time. There is no event, however important to us, which he has exempted from the general laws that govern the universe, or which he has peculiarly reserved for his own immediate action and operation. The revolution of states and empires depends upon the smallest caprice or passion of single men; and the lives of men are shortened or extended by the smallest accident of air or diet, sunshine or tempest. Nature still continues her progress and operation; and if general laws be ever broke by particular volitions of the Deity, it is after a manner which entirely escapes human observation. As, on the one hand, the elements and other inanimate parts of the creation carry on their action without regard to the particular interest and situation of men; so men are entrusted to their own judgment and discretion in the various shocks of matter, and may employ every faculty with which they are endowed, in order to provide for their ease, happiness, or preservation. What is the meaning then of that principle, that a man, who, tired of life, and hunted by pain and misery, bravely overcomes all the natural terrors of death, and makes his escape from this cruel scene; that such a man, I say, has incurred the indignation of his Creator, by encroaching on the office of divine providence, and disturbing the order of the universe? Shall we assert, that the Almighty has reserved to himself, in any peculiar manner, the disposal of the lives of men, and has not submitted that event, in common with others, to the general laws by which the universe is governed? This is plainly false: the lives of men depend upon the same laws as the lives of all other animals; and these are subjected to the general laws of matter and motion. The fall of a tower, or the infusion of a poison, will destroy a man equally with the meanest creature; an inundation sweeps away every thing without distinction that comes within the reach of its fury. Since therefore the lives of men are forever dependent on the general laws of matter and motion, is a man's disposing of his life criminal, because in every case it is criminal to encroach upon these laws, or disturb their operation? But this seems absurd: all animals are entrusted to their own prudence and skill for their conduct in the world; and have full authority, as far as their power extends, to alter all the operations of nature. Without the exercise of this authority, they could not subsist a moment; every action, every motion of a man, innovates on the order of some parts of matter, and diverts from their ordinary course the general laws of motion. Putting together therefore these conclusions, we find that human life depends upon the general laws of matter and motion, and that it is no encroachment on the office of Providence to disturb or alter these general laws: has not everyone of consequence the free disposal of his own life? And may he not lawfully employ that power with which nature has endowed him? In order to destroy the evidence of this conclusion, we must show a reason why this particular case is excepted. Is it because human life is of such great importance, that it is a presumption for human prudence to dispose of it? But the life of a man is of no greater importance to the universe than that of an oyster: and were it of ever so great importance, the order of human nature has actually submitted it to human prudence, and reduced us to a necessity, in every incident, of determining concerning it.

Were the disposal of human life so much reserved as the peculiar province of the Almighty, that it were an encroachment on his right for men to dispose of their own lives, it would be equally criminal to act for the preservation of life as for its destruction. If I turn aside a stone which is falling upon my head, I disturb the course of nature; and I invade the peculiar province of the Almighty, by lengthening out my life beyond the period, which, by the general laws of matter and motion, he had assigned it.

A hair, a fly, an insect, is able to destroy this mighty being whose life is of such importance. Is it an absurdity to suppose that human prudence may lawfully dispose of what depends on such insignificant causes? It would be no crime in me to divert the Nile or Danube from its course, were I able to effect such purposes. Where then is the crime of turning a few ounces of blood from their natural channel? Do you imagine that I repine at Providence, or curse my creation, because I go out of life, and put a period to a being which, were it to continue, would render me miserable? Far be such sentiments from me. I am only convinced of a matter of fact which you yourself acknowledge possible, that human life may be unhappy; and that my existence, if further prolonged, would become ineligible: but I thank Providence, both for the good which I have already enjoyed, and for the power with which I am endowed of escaping the ills that threaten me.[2] To you it belongs to repine at Providence, who foolishly imagine that you have no such power; and who must still prolong a hated life, though loaded with pain and sickness, with shame and poverty. Do not you teach, that when any ill befalls me, though by the malice of my enemies, I ought to be resigned to Providence; and that the actions of men are the operations of the Almighty, as much as the actions of inanimate beings? When I fall upon my own sword, therefore, I receive my death equally from the hands of the Deity as if it had proceeded from a lion, a precipice, or a fever. The submission which you require to Providence, in every calamity that befalls me, excludes not human skill and industry, if possibly by their means I can avoid or escape the calamity. And why may I not employ one remedy as well as another? If my life be not my own, it were criminal for me to put it in danger, as well as to dispose of it; nor could one man deserve the appellation of *hero,* whom glory or friendship transports into the greatest dangers;

and another merit the reproach of *wretch* or *miscreant,* who puts a period to his life from the same or like motives. There is no being which possesses any power or faculty, that it receives not from its Creator; nor is there anyone, which by ever so irregular an action, can encroach upon the plan of his providence, or disorder the universe. Its operations are his works equally with that chain of events which it invades; and whichever principle prevails, we may for that very reason conclude it to be most favored by him. Be it animate or inanimate; rational or irrational; it is all the same case: its power is still derived from the Supreme Creator, and is alike comprehended in the order of his providence. When the horror of pain prevails over the love of life; when a voluntary action anticipates the effects of blind causes; it is only in consequence of those powers and principles which he has implanted in his creatures. Divine Providence is still inviolate, and placed far beyond the reach of human injuries.[3] It is impious, says the old Roman superstition, to divert rivers from their course, or invade the prerogatives of nature. It is impious, says the French superstition, to inoculate for the smallpox, or usurp the business of Providence, by voluntarily producing distempers and maladies. It is impious, says the modern European superstition, to put a period to our own life, and thereby rebel against our Creator: and why not impious, say I, to build houses, cultivate the ground, or sail upon the ocean? In all these actions we employ our powers of mind and body to produce some innovation in the course of nature; and in none of them do we any more. They are all of them therefore equally innocent, or equally criminal. *But you are placed by Providence, like a sentinel, in a particular station; and when you desert it without being recalled, you are equally guilty of rebellion against your Almighty Sovereign, and have incurred his displeasure*—I ask, Why do you conclude that Providence has placed me in this station? For my part, I find that I owe my birth to a long chain of causes, of which many depended upon voluntary actions of men. *But Providence guided all these causes, and nothing happens in the universe without its consent and cooperation.* If so, then neither does my death, however voluntary, happen without its consent; and whenever pain or sorrow so far overcome my patience, as to make me tired of life, I may conclude that I am recalled from my station in the clearest and most express terms. It is Providence surely that has placed me at this present moment in this chamber: but may I not leave it when I think proper, without being liable to the imputation of having deserted my post or station? When I shall be dead, the principles of which I am composed will still perform their part in the universe, and will be equally useful in the grand fabric, as when they compose this individual creature. The difference to the whole will be no greater than betwixt my being in a chamber and in the open air. The one change is of more importance to me than the other; but not more so to the universe.

It is a kind of blasphemy to imagine that any created being can disturb the order of the world, or invade the business of Providence? It supposes, that that being possesses powers and faculties which it received not from its Creator, and which are not subordinate to his government and authority. A man may disturb society, no doubt, and thereby incur the displeasure of the Almighty: but the government of the world is placed far beyond his reach and violence. And how does it appear that the Almighty is displeased with those actions that disturb society? By the principles which he has implanted in human nature, and which inspire us with a sentiment of remorse if we ourselves have been guilty of such actions, and with that of blame and disapprobation, if we ever observe them in others. Let us now examine, according to the method proposed, whether Suicide be of this kind of actions, and be a breach of our duty to our *neighbor* and to *society*.

A man who retires from life does no harm to society: he only ceases to do good; which, if it is an injury, is of the lowest kind. All our obligations to do good to society seem to imply something reciprocal. I receive the benefits of society, and therefore ought to promote its interests; but when I withdraw myself altogether from society, can I be bound any longer? But allowing that our obligations to do good were perpetual, they have certainly some bounds; I am not obliged to do a small good to society at the expense of a great harm to myself: why then should I prolong a miserable existence, because of some frivolous advantage which the public may perhaps receive from me? If upon account of age and infirmities, I may lawfully resign any office, and employ my time altogether in fencing against these calamaties, and alleviating as much as possible the miseries of my future life; why may I not cut short these miseries at once by an action which is no more prejudicial to society? But suppose that it is no longer in my power to promote the interest of society; suppose that I am a burden to it; suppose that my life hinders some person from being much more useful to society: in such cases, my resignation of life must not only be innocent, but laudable. And most people who lie under any temptation to abandon existence, are in some such situation; those who have health, or power, or authority, have commonly better reason to be in humor with the world.

A man is engaged in a conspiracy for the public interest; is seized upon suspicion; is threatened with the rack; and knows from his own weakness that the secret will be extorted from him: could such a one consult the public interest better than by putting a quick period to a miserable life? This was the case of the famous and brave Strozzi of Florence.[4] Again, suppose a malefactor is justly condemned to a shameful death; can any reason be imagined why he may not anticipate his punishment, and save himself all the anguish of thinking on its dreadful approaches? He invades the business of Providence no more than the magistrate did who ordered his execution; and his voluntary death is equally advantageous to society, by ridding it of a pernicious member.

That Suicide may often be consistent with interest and with our duty to ourselves, no one can question, who allows that age, sickness, or misfortune, may render life a burden, and make it worse even than annihilation. I believe that no man ever threw away life while it was worth keeping. For such is our natural horror of death, that small motives will never be able to reconcile us to it; and though perhaps the situation of a man's health or fortune did not seem to require this remedy; we may at least be assured, that anyone who, without apparent reason, has had recourse to it, was cursed with such an incurable depravity or gloominess of temper as must poison all enjoyment, and render him equally miserable as if he had been loaded with the most grievous misfortunes. If Suicide be supposed a crime, it is only cowardice can impel us to it. If it be no crime, both prudence and courage should engage us to rid ourselves at once of existence when it becomes a burden. It is the only way that we can then be useful to society, by setting an example, which, if imitated, would preserve to everyone his chance for happiness in life and would effectually free him from all danger or misery.[5]

NOTES

1. Cicero, *De Divinatione* [II. 149–50.]
2. Agamus Deo gratias, quod nemo in vita teneri potest. Seneca, *Epistles* XII. 10.
3. Tacitus, *Annals* I. 74.
4. [Filippo Strozzi (1488–1538), wealthy Florentine merchant, captured after organizing an abortive revolt against Cosimo de' Medici. He was not strong, and incapable of withstanding torture; one day he was found dead in his cell, lying between two bloodstained swords, with a note that read in part: "If I have

not hitherto known how to live, I will know how to die." Unfortunately for Hume's argument, it is now believed that Cosimo staged the "suicide" to rid himself of his enemy.]

5. It would be easy to prove that suicide is as lawful under the Christian dispensation as it was to the Heathens. There is not a single text of Scripture which prohibits it. That great and infallible rule of faith and practice which must control all philosophy and human reasoning, has left us in this particular to our natural liberty. Resignation to Providence is indeed recommended in Scripture; but that implies only submission to ills that are unavoidable, not to such as may be remedied by prudence or courage. *Thou shalt not kill,* is evidently meant to exclude only the killing of others, over whose life we have no authority. That this precept, like most of the Scripture precepts, must be modified by reason and common sense, is plain from the practice of magistrates, who punish criminals capitally, notwithstanding the letter of the law. But were the commandment ever to express against suicide, it would now have no authority, for all the law of *Moses* is abolished, except so far as it is established by the law of nature. And we have already endeavored to prove that suicide is not prohibited by that law. In all cases Christians and Heathens are precisely upon the same footing; *Cato* and *Brutus, Arrea* and *Portia* acted heroically; those who now imitate their example ought to receive the same praises from posterity. The power of committing suicide is regarded by *Pliny* as an advantage which men possess even above the Deity himself. "Deus non sibi potest mortem consciscere si velit, quod homini dedit optimum in tantis vitae poenis." [*Natural History,* II. 5.]

4

Duties towards the Body in Regard to Life

Immanuel Kant

What are our powers of disposal over our life? Have we any authority of disposal over it in any shape or form? How far is it incumbent upon us to take care of it? These are questions which fall to be considered in connection with our duties towards the body in regard to life. We must, however, by way of introduction, make the following observations. If the body were related to life not as a condition but as an accident or circumstance so that we could at will divest ourselves of it; if we could slip out of it and slip into another just as we leave one country for another, then the body would be subject to our free will and we could rightly have the disposal of it. This, however, would not imply that we could similarly dispose of our life, but only of our circumstances, of the movable goods, the furniture of life. In fact, however, our life is entirely conditioned by our body, so that we cannot conceive of a life not mediated by the body and we cannot make use of our freedom except through the body. It is, therefore, obvious that the body constitutes a part of ourselves. If a man destroys his body, and so his life, he does it by the use of his will, which is itself destroyed in the process. But to use the power of a

From *Lectures in Ethics,* trans. Louis Infield (New York: Harper & Row, 1963), pp. 147–57. Reprinted by permission of Routledge, Chapman & Hall, Inc., Publishers.

free will for its own destruction is self-contradictory. If freedom is the condition of life it cannot be employed to abolish life and so to destroy and abolish itself. To use life for its own destruction, to use life for producing lifelessness, is self-contradictory. These preliminary remarks are sufficient to show that man cannot rightly have any power of disposal in regard to himself and his life, but only in regard to his circumstances. His body gives man power over his life; were he a spirit he could not destroy his life; life in the absolute has been invested by nature with indestructibility and is an end in itself; hence it follows that man cannot have the power to dispose of his life.

SUICIDE

Suicide can be regarded in various lights; it might be held to be reprehensible, or permissible, or even heroic. In the first place we have the specious view that suicide can be allowed and tolerated. Its advocates argue thus. So long as he does not violate the proprietary rights of others, man is a free agent. With regard to his body there are various things he can properly do; he can have a boil lanced or a limb amputated, and disregard a scar; he is, in fact, free to do whatever he may consider useful and advisable. If then he comes to the conclusion that the most useful and advisable thing that he can do is to put an end to his life, why should he not be entitled to do so? Why not, if he sees that he can no longer go on living and that he will be ridding himself of misfortune, torment, and disgrace? To be sure he robs himself of a full life, but he escapes once and for all from calamity and misfortune. The argument sounds most plausible. But let us, leaving aside religious considerations, examine the act itself. We may treat our body as we please, provided our motives are those of self-preservation. If, for instance, his foot is a hindrance to life, a man might have it amputated. To preserve his person he has the right of disposal over his body. But in taking his life he does not preserve his person; he disposes of his person and not of its attendant circumstances; he robs himself of his person. This is contrary to the highest duty we have towards ourselves, for it annuls the condition of all other duties; it goes beyond the limits of the use of free will, for this use is possible only through the existence of the Subject.

There is another set of considerations which make suicide seem plausible. A man might find himself so placed that he can continue living only under circumstances which deprive life of all value; in which he can no longer live conformably to virtue and prudence, so that he must from noble motives put an end to his life. The advocates of this view quote in support of it the example of Cato. Cato knew that the entire Roman nation relied upon him in their resistance to Caesar, but he found that he could not prevent himself from falling into Caesar's hands. What was he to do? If he, the champion of freedom, submitted, everyone would say, "If Cato himself submits, what else can we do?" If, on the other hand, he killed himself, his death might spur on the Romans to fight to the bitter end in defense of their freedom. So he killed himself. He thought that it was necessary for him to die. He thought that if he could not go on living as Cato, he could not go on living at all. It must certainly be admitted that in a case such as this, where suicide is a virtue, appearances are in its favor. But this is the only example which has given the world the opportunity of defending suicide. It is the only example of its kind and there has been no similar case since. Lucretia also killed herself, but on grounds of modesty and in a fury of vengeance. It is obviously our duty to preserve our honor, particularly in relation to the opposite sex, for whom it is a merit; but we must endeavor to save our honor only to this extent, that we ought not to surrender it for selfish and lustful purposes. To do what Lucretia did is to adopt a remedy which is not at our disposal; it would have been better had she defended her honor unto death; that would not have been suicide and would have been right; for it is no suicide to risk one's life against one's enemies, and even to sacrifice it, in order to observe one's duties towards oneself.

No one under the sun can bind me to commit suicide; no sovereign can do so. The sovereign can call upon his subjects to fight to the death for their country, and those who fall on the field of battle are not suicides, but the victims of fate. Not only is this not suicide; but the opposite, a faint heart and fear of the death which threatens by the necessity of fate, is no true self-preservation; for he who runs away to save his own life, and leaves his comrades in the lurch, is a coward; but he who defends himself and his fellows even unto death is no suicide, but noble and high-minded; for life is not to be highly regarded for its own sake. I should endeavor to preserve my own life only so far as I am worthy to live. We must draw a distinction between the suicide and the victim of fate. A man who shortens his life by intemperance is guilty of imprudence and indirectly of his own death; but his guilt is not direct; he did not intend to kill himself; his death was not premeditated. For all our offenses are either *culpa* or *dolus*. There is certainly no *dolus* here, but there is *culpa*; and we can say of such a man that he was guilty of his own death, but we cannot say of him that he is a suicide. What constitutes suicide is the intention to destroy oneself. Intemperance and excess which shorten life ought not, therefore, to be called suicide; for if we raise intemperance to the level of suicide, we lower suicide to the level of intemperance. Imprudence, which does not imply a desire to cease to live, must, therefore, be distinguished from the intention to murder oneself. Serious violations of our duty towards ourselves produce an aversion accompanied either by horror or by disgust; suicide is of the horrible kind, *crimina carnis* of the disgusting. We shrink in horror from suicide because all nature seeks its own preservation; an injured tree, a living body, an animal does so; how then could man make of his freedom, which is the acme of life and constitutes its worth, a principle for his own destruction? Nothing more terrible can be imagined; for if man were on every occasion master of his own life, he would be master of the lives of others; and being ready to sacrifice his life at any and every time rather than be captured, he would perpetrate every conceivable crime and vice. We are, therefore, horrified at the very thought of suicide; by it man sinks lower than the beasts; we look upon a suicide as carrion, whilst our sympathy goes forth to the victim of fate.

Those who advocate suicide seek to give the widest interpretation to freedom. There is something flattering in the thought that we can take our own life if we are so minded; and so we find even right-thinking persons defending suicide in this respect. There are many circumstances under which life ought to be sacrificed. If I cannot preserve my life except by violating my duties towards myself, I am bound to sacrifice my life rather than violate these duties. But suicide is in no circumstances permissible. Humanity in one's own person is something inviolable; it is a holy trust; man is master of all else, but he must not lay hands upon himself. A being who existed of his own necessity could not possibly destroy himself; a being whose existence is not necessary must regard life as the condition of everything else, and in the consciousness that life is a trust reposed in him, such a being recoils at the thought of committing a breach of his holy trust by turning his life against himself. Man can only dispose over things; beasts are things in this sense; but man is not a thing, not a beast. If he disposes over himself, he treats his value as that of a beast. He who so behaves, who has no respect for human nature and makes a thing of himself, becomes for everyone an Object of freewill. We are free to treat him as a beast, as a thing, and to use him for our sport as we do a horse or a dog, for he is no longer a human being; he has made a thing of himself, and, having himself discarded his humanity, he cannot expect that others should respect humanity in him. Yet humanity is worthy of esteem. Even when a man is a bad man, humanity in his person is worthy of esteem. Suicide is not abominable and inadmissible because life should be highly prized; were it so, we could each have our own opinion of how highly we should prize it, and the rule of prudence would often indicate suicide as the best means. But the rule of morality does not admit of it under any condition because it degrades human nature below the level of animal nature and so destroys it. Yet there is much in the world far more important than life. To observe morality is far more important. It is better to sacrifice one's life than one's morality. To live is not a necessity; but to live honorably while life lasts is a necessity. We can at all times go on living and doing our duty towards ourselves without having to do violence to ourselves. But he who is prepared to take his own life is no longer worthy to live at all. The pragmatic ground of impulse to live is happiness. Can I then take my own life because I cannot live happily? No! It is not necessary that whilst I live I should live happily; but it is necessary that so long as I live I should live honorably. Misery gives no right to any man to take his own life, for then we should all be entitled to take our lives for lack of pleasure. All our duties towards ourselves would then be directed towards pleasure; but the fulfillment of those duties may demand that we should even sacrifice our life.

Is suicide heroic or cowardly? Sophistication, even though well meant, is not a good thing. It is not good to defend either virtue or vice by splitting hairs. Even right-thinking people declaim against suicide on wrong lines. They say that it is arrant cowardice. But instances of suicide of great heroism exist. We cannot, for example, regard the suicides of Cato and of Atticus as cowardly. Rage, passion, and insanity are the most frequent causes of suicide, and that is why persons who attempt suicide and are saved from it are so terrified at their own act that they do not dare to repeat the attempt. There was a time in Roman and in Greek history when suicide was regarded as honorable, so much so that the Romans forbade their slaves to commit suicide because they did not belong to themselves but to their masters and so were regarded as things, like all other animals. The Stoics said that suicide is the sage's peaceful death; he leaves the world as he might leave a smoky room for another, because it no longer pleases him; he leaves the world, not because he is no longer happy in it, but because he disdains it. It has already been mentioned that man is greatly flattered by the idea that he is free to remove himself from this world, if he so wishes. He may not make use of this freedom, but the thought of possessing it pleases him. It seems even to have a moral aspect, for if man is capable of removing himself from the world at his own will, he need not submit to anyone; he can retain his independence and tell the rudest truths to the cruellest of tyrants. Torture cannot bring him to heel, because he can leave the world at a moment's notice as a free man can leave the country, if and when he wills it. But this semblance of morality vanishes as soon as we see that man's freedom cannot subsist except on a condition which is immutable. The condition is that man may not use his freedom against himself to his own destruction, but that, on the contrary, he should allow nothing external to limit it. Freedom thus conditioned is noble. No chance or misfortune ought to make us afraid to live; we ought to go on living as long as we can do so as human beings and honorably. To bewail one's fate and misfortune is in itself dishonorable. Had Cato faced any torments which Caesar might have inflicted upon him with a resolute mind and remained steadfast, it would have been noble of him; to violate himself was not so. Those who advocate suicide and teach that there is authority for it necessarily do much harm in a republic of free men. Let us imagine a state in which men held as a general opinion that they were entitled to commit suicide, and that there was even merit and honor in so doing. How dreadful everyone would find them. For he who does not respect his life even in principle cannot be restrained from the most dreadful vices; he recks neither king nor torments.

But as soon as we examine suicide from the standpoint of religion we immediately see it in its true light. We have been placed in this world under certain conditions and for specific purposes. But a suicide opposes the purpose of his Creator; he arrives in the other world as one who has deserted his post; he must be looked upon as a rebel against God. So long as we remember the truth that it is God's intention to preserve life, we are bound to regulate our activities in conformity with it. We have no right to offer violence to our nature's powers of self-preservation and to upset the wisdom of her arrangements. This duty is upon us until the time comes when God expressly commands us to leave this life. Human beings are sentinels on earth and may not leave their posts until relieved by another beneficent hand. God is our owner; we are His property; His providence works for our good. A bondman in the care of a beneficent master deserves punishment if he opposes his master's wishes.

But suicide is not inadmissible and abominable because God has forbidden it; God has forbidden it because it is abominable in that it degrades man's inner worth below that of the animal creation. Moral philosophers must, therefore, first and foremost show that suicide is abominable. We find, as a rule, that those who labor for their happiness are more liable to suicide; having tasted the refinements of pleasure, and being deprived of them, they give way to grief, sorrow, and melancholy.

CARE FOR ONE'S LIFE

We are in duty bound to take care of our life; but in this connection it must be remarked that life, in and for itself, is not the greatest of the gifts entrusted to our keeping and of which we must take care. There are duties which are far greater than life and which can often be fulfilled only by sacrificing life. Observation and experience show that a worthless man values his life more than his person. He who has no inner worth sets greater store by his life; but he who has a greater inner worth places a lesser value upon his life. The latter would sacrifice his life rather than be guilty of a disgraceful action; he values his person more than his life. But a man of no inner worth would act basely rather than sacrifice his life. He certainly preserves his life, but he is no longer worthy to live; he has, in his person, disgraced human nature and its dignity. But is it consistent that the man who places a lesser value upon his life should command a greater value in his person? There is something obscure about this, though the fact is clear enough. Man looks upon life, which consists in the union of the soul with the body, as a contingent thing, and rightly so. The principle of free action in him is of a kind which insists that life, which consists in the union of soul and body, should be held in low esteem. Let us take an example. Assume that a number of persons are innocently accused of treachery, and that whilst some of them are truly honorable, others, although innocent of the particular accusation leveled against them, are contemptible and of no real worth; assume further that they are all sentenced together, and that each of them has to choose between death and penal servitude for life; it is certain that the honorable amongst them would choose death, and the vile ones the galleys. A man of inner worth does not shrink from death; he would die rather than live as an object of contempt, a member of a gang of scoundrels in the galleys; but the worthless man prefers the galleys, almost as if they were his proper place. Thus there exist duties to which life must be subordinated, and in order to fulfill them we must give no countenance to cowardice and fears for our life. Man's cowardice dishonors humanity. It is cowardly to place a high value upon physical life. The man who on every trifling occasion fears for his life makes a laughing-stock of himself. We must await death with resolution. That must be of little importance which it is of great importance to despise.

On the other hand we ought not to risk our life and hazard losing it for interested and private purposes. To do so is not only imprudent but base. It would, for instance, be wrong to wager for a large sum of money that we would swim across some great river. There is no material benefit in life so great that we should regard it as a duty to risk our life for it. But circumstances do exist in which men risk their lives from motives of interest. A soldier does so in the wars; but his motives are not of private interest, but of the general good. But seeing that human beings are so constituted that they war against each other, men are to be found who devote themselves to war merely as a profession. How far we should value our life, and how far we may risk it, is a very subtle question. It turns on the following considerations. Humanity in our own person is an object of the highest esteem and is inviolable in us; rather than dishonor it, or allow it to be dishonored, man ought to sacrifice his life; for can he himself hold his manhood in honor if it is to be dishonored by others? If a man cannot preserve his life except by dishonoring his humanity, he ought rather to sacrifice it; it is true that he endangers his animal life but he can feel that, so long as he lived, he lived honorably. How long he lives is of no account; it is not his life that he loses, but only the prolongation of his years, for nature has already decreed that he must die at some time; what matters is that, so long as he lives, man should live honorably and should not disgrace the dignity of humanity; if he can no longer live honorably, he cannot live at all; his moral life is at an end. The moral life is at an end if it is no longer in keeping with the dignity of humanity. Through all the ills and torments of life the path of morality is determined. No matter what torments I have to suffer, I can live morally. I must suffer them all, including the torments of death, rather than commit a disgraceful action. The moment I can no longer live in honor but become unworthy of life by such an action, I can no longer live at all. Thus it is far better to die honored and respected than to prolong one's life for a few years by a disgraceful act and go on living a rogue. If, for instance, a woman cannot preserve her life any longer except by surrendering her person to the will of another, she is bound to give up her life rather than dishonor humanity in her own person, which is what she would be doing in giving herself up as a thing to the will of another.

The preservation of one's life is, therefore, not the highest duty, and men must often give up their lives merely to secure that they shall have lived honorably. There are many instances of this; and although lawyers may argue that to preserve life is the highest duty and that *in casu necessitatis* a man is bound to stand up for his life, yet this is no matter of jurisprudence. Jurisprudence should concern itself only with man's duties to his neighbor, with what is lawful and unlawful, but not with duties towards oneself; it cannot force a man on any occasion to give up his life; for how could it force him? Only by taking his life from him. Of course, lawyers must regard the preservation of life as the highest duty, because the threat of death is their most powerful weapon in examining a man. In any event, there is no *casus necessitatis* except where morality relieves me of the duty to take care of my life. Misery, danger, and torture are no *casus necessitatis* for perserving my life. Necessity cannot cancel morality. If, then, I cannot preserve my life except by disgraceful conduct, virtue relieves me of this duty because a higher duty here comes into play and commands me to sacrifice my life.

5

Did Socrates Commit Suicide?

R. G. Frey

It is rarely, if at all, thought that Socrates committed suicide; but such was the case, or so I want to suggest. My suggestion turns not upon any new interpretation of ancient sources but rather upon seeking a determination of the concept of suicide itself.

Suppose Sir Percy is cleaning his gun, and that his finger slips on to the trigger, as a result of which the gun discharges, mortally wounding him: does Sir Percy commit suicide? It seems reasonably clear that he does not: if killing oneself is a part of committing suicide, it is not the whole. What seems wanted is a reference to the fact that Percy did not intend to take his life; it is killing oneself intentionally, or self-murder, and not self-killing, that constitutes suicide. If this is so, then Socrates (I mean the Socrates of Plato's *Phaedo*) did plainly commit suicide. For he drank the hemlock knowingly, not unknowingly or in ignorance of what it was or what its effect on him would be, and intentionally, not accidentally or mistakenly; and he died as a result of his act of drinking the hemlock.

From *Philosophy* 53 (1978): 106–108. © Copyright Royal Institute of Philosophy. Reprinted with the permission of Cambridge University Press.

A number of ways in which one might try to avoid this conclusion come to mind; but each of them, I think, fails.

"Socrates did not want to die." This is not so very obvious. It is apparent from Plato's narrative of Socrates's last hours with Phaedo and his friends that Socrates intends to drink the hemlock. At least ordinarily, however, an agent intends an act only if he knows he is doing it and wants to do it either as an end in itself or as a means to some further end. So unless one is prepared to say that Socrates did not intend to drink the hemlock, we can infer from the fact that he intended to drink it, together with his knowledge of what its effect on him would be, that he wanted to die. (It should perhaps be added, too, that in the early passages of the *Phaedo,* where Socrates expounds his view of what the philosopher's attitude toward death should be [61c–69e], he does betray a wish to die.)

"Socrates was forced to drink the hemlock." This is simply untrue. He did not take the cup of hemlock reluctantly. Nor, after he had taken it, did he throw its contents to the floor. He did not drink the hemlock against his will: his jailers were not required to listen to his protests or pleas, and they did not have to hold him down and pour the hemlock down his throat. Even granted that he had to die, Socrates had a choice between drinking the hemlock willingly and having it, so to speak, force-fed; and only by choosing to be force-fed would Socrates have been forced to drink the hemlock, that is, compelled to die against his will.

"Socrates was under duress." Even if true, this fact is irrelevant, unless one is prepared to argue, what is almost certainly false, that duress vitiates choice. Socrates had to die, but he could die by his own hand, by taking and drinking the hemlock willingly, or by the hand of another, by having the hemlock force-fed. What duress Socrates is under pertains to his having to die, not to his having to die by his own hand.

"The whole context in which Socrates drinks the hemlock, namely, his trial, the verdict, and the drinking of hemlock as his sentence, is what is important; he does not commit suicide because he takes the hemlock in the context of an execution by the state of Athens." I agree that Socrates takes the hemlock as a result of his sentence, indeed, as his sentence, but I deny that intentionally taking one's life because it is one's sentence *ipso facto* precludes committing suicide. Suppose that the sentence for murder were a bit different, that every convicted murderer was allowed to live for twelve months from the date on which his sentence was passed, and could either take his own life within this period or else face the absolute certainty of a state execution at the end of twelve months: do not the murderers who intentionally take their own lives commit suicide? The fact that their sentence is as it is does not preclude their doing so; on the contrary, given that they have to die, they intentionally take their own lives and thereby make plain their decisions to commit suicide rather than to undergo state executions. True, their acts of intentionally taking their own lives can be described as "implementing their sentence" as well as "committing suicide"; but the use of the former description in no way bars the use of the latter to describe what they did.

"The time of Socrates's death is fixed by his sentence, and this is what is important; he does not commit suicide because he does not choose when to die." The assumption that choosing the time and moment of death is part of what it is to commit suicide is false. Suppose Sir Percy decides to commit suicide but simply cannot face cutting his wrists or shooting himself in the temple; instead, he plants hundreds of pounds of gelignite under his house and attaches the fuses to his telephone, so that, if his telephone rings, his house explodes; and then he sits down to wait. Percy will die whenever his telephone rings, but *he* does not know or determine (or perhaps even care) when that will be; and if, unknown to him, his telephone has been disconnected, then it may never ring. But if at some time or other it does ring, and if Percy does die, he has certainly committed suicide. Again, Captain Oates was aware that, in walking away from Scott's camp, he was walking to his death; and he could have been reasonably certain of dying soon. But he did not know or choose the moment of death, and in reaching his decision to walk away, I doubt if he cared just *when* death would come. Thus the fact that Socrates does not choose the time and moment of his death does not *ipso facto* preclude his committing suicide.

"Socrates died a noble and dignified death and suicide is ignoble and undignified." On the contrary; the fact that Socrates died a noble and dignified death does not show that he did not commit suicide, but rather that suicide need not be ignoble and undignified.

6

Attitudes toward Suicide

Joseph Fletcher

Most of us know that anthropologists have found every imaginable attitude toward suicide in both savage and civilized societies. Anthropologists, however, like psychiatrists and sociologists, are able only to provide us with data; in their scientific capacity they cannot jump the gap between what is and what ought to be. To suppose that tabulating moral sentiments described from observation settles an ethical question is what is called the naturalistic fallacy—confusing what is with what ought to be. Whether we ought to be free to end our lives or not is a question of philosophy, of ethics in particular. If a psychiatrist, for example, asserts or implies that people ought not to choose naughtness or oblivionate themselves (to use Herman Melville's neologisms), that scientist is wearing a philosopher's hat. *Ought* is not in the scientific lexicon.

In spite of the defiant immortalists who look forward to resurrection by cryonics or by outwitting cell death biochemically (such as Alan Harrington, who stated, "Death is an imposition on the human race, and no longer acceptable"), we know perfectly well that aging is a fatal disease and we all are its victims. The ethical question is whether we may ever

Originally published as "In Defense of Suicide," in *Suizid und Euthanasie,* edited by Albin Eser (Stuttgart: Ferdinand Enke Verlag, 1976), pp. 233–44. Reprinted by permission.

rightly take any rational human initiative in death and dying or are, instead, obliged in conscience to look upon life and death fatalistically, as something that just has to happen to us willy-nilly.

We have pretty well settled the life-control issue with our contraceptive practices and policies; now we must look just as closely at the death-control problem. If we may initiate life, may we not terminate it? Were Ernest Hemingway and his father before him wrong to shoot themselves? Ethically? Psychologically?

THE ETHICAL QUESTION

Speaking as we are from the vantage point of moral philosophy, we must begin with the postulate that no action is intrinsically right or wrong, that nothing is inherently good or evil. Right and wrong, good and evil, desirable and undesirable—all are ethical terms and all are predicates, not properties. The moral "value" of any human act is always contingent, depending on the shape of the action in the situation—*Sitz im Leben* or *Situationsethik*. The variables and factors in each set of circumstances are the determinants of what ought to be done—not prefabricated generalizations or prescriptive rules. Clinical analysis and flexibility are indispensable. No "law" of conduct is always obliging; what we ought to do is whatever maximizes human well-being.

It is essential to grasp the difference between moral values and behavioral norms. Only in this way will we understand why our values are a priori while our actions should be flexibly selective and not legalistic or rule-bound. We might say that our opinions about what is good are subjective and visceral; our judgments about what we ought to do about what we feel is good are more objective and cerebral.

There simply is no way to "prove" our values by logic; they are established by a mixture of conditioning, choice, and commitment. As Ludwig Wittgenstein saw the problem, "This is a terrible business—just terrible. You can at best stammer when you talk of it."

On the other hand, when acting as moral agents, tailoring our deeds to fit our values and ideals, we have to use logic and critical reason, especially when we have to decide which value gets priority in cases of competing values. For example, if truth telling has a high-order value but conflicts with a therapeutic goal, telling the truth might sometimes be the wrong thing to do.

To suppose that we would always be obliged to follow any rule of conduct is only tenable on a metaphysical basis or because of an alleged revelation of eternal absolutes. Such universals are what the Greeks called the *proton pseudon,* the basic error of conventional (that is, unexamined) moralism. Most Christian and many Jewish moralists use starting points of this kind. Without such a supernatural support, however, any attempt to assign intrinsic moral value to anything—truth, chastity, property, health, or even life itself—is an abysmal ethical mistake.

Stepping for a moment into another context, we can clarify the point at stake by quoting a question-and-answer column in a religious magazine: "*Q.* My wife is sterile but wants her 'marital rights.' I have a contagious venereal disease. May I wear a prophylactic sheath? *A.* No. Even though she could not conceive and you would infect her, contraceptive intercourse is an intrinsically evil act." The situation makes no difference. The end sought makes no difference. The good consequences make no difference. Nothing makes any difference. The act itself is wrong. This is the essence of "intrinsic" morality.

The typical moral theologian, for example, whose ethics prohibit suicide as such, would condemn a captured soldier's committing suicide to avoid betraying his comrades under torture—because suicide is held to be an evil act in itself, like Kant's *Ding-an-sich,* a defiance of the will of God. An empirical or clinical ethic, being without that kind of dogmatic sanction, would have to agree that suicide can be right sometimes, wrong sometimes.

A slight variant on saying "suicide is not right" is saying "we have no right" to end our lives by choice. People are always mixing human "rights" and right conduct together. In a humanistic ethics, when suicide helps human beings it is right. That is, we have a right to do it. What makes it right is human need. Human rights are not self-validating, not intrinsically valid. It is need that validates rights, not the other way around. When rights are asserted over or cut across human needs, we are faced with a set of superhuman moral principles that often can be callous and cruel contractions of a humane morality.

SOME HISTORY

William Shakespeare put the ethical question this way: "Then is it sin / To rush into the secret house of death / Ere death dare come to us?"

Antony and Cleopatra IV, XV:80–82. Cassio, though a good Catholic, thought Othello's suicide was noble. In *Romeo and Juliet* the priest did not condemn the self-conclusion chosen by the young lovers. Shakespeare never expressed the kind of moralistic horror we find in Dante, who put suicides in the Seventh Circle of Hell, lower than murderers and heretics. As a matter of fact, few cultures or traditions have condemned suicide out of whole cloth, indiscriminately.

Suicide poses an ethical issue that is ultimately a matter of values and how we reason about them. The story of what various people have thought and done about suicide does not settle the problem of what is right and good about it. Even so, the pages of history tell us things that help us to put the ethics of elective death in perspective, and we will look at the record in capsule.

Europe, Asia, Africa, America—all tell much the same story. Suicide is seen as absurd and tragic, noble and mean, brave and cowardly, sane and silly; every way of judging it has been taken. Some of the religious and superstitious have condemned it wholesale; others have even praised it. For example, the Koran holds that suicide interferes with kismet, Allah's control of life and destiny, making it therefore much more to be condemned than homicide. Cardinal Richelieu expressed a similar idea. Some cultures, on the other hand, have honored suicides; the American Indians endured genocide at the hands of the Christian conquistadors Cortez and Pizarro even while their Spanish priests were condemning the Indians' selective suicide.

The Japanese honor the rite of seppuku, or hara-kiri, and the Hindus honor suttee. Buddhist monks who used self-immolation to protest Thieu's dictatorship in South Vietnam are another example.

The Buddhist admiration for kamikaze is more complicated ethically because suicidal practices of that order combine killing oneself with killing others. Something like banzai is to be seen in the suicidal commando tactics of Palestinian guerrillas and in the "living bomb" gestures of Viet Cong terrorists. The supposed difference between comitting suicide in banzai and volunteering to fly in the Luftwaffe or the RAF during the Battle of Britain pose an interesting analysis problem—speaking ethically, not psychiatrically.

More primitive peoples often believed that a suicide's soul or ghost would wander around without a resting place, haunting the living. To prevent this, medieval Christians buried a suicide with a stake through the heart and dug the grave at a crossroads instead of in "hallowed" (blessed) ground to keep it from poisoning the soil. The Baganda people used a similar defense strategy, as the storied missionary Livingstone discovered when he stayed among them. The Alabama Indians threw the bodies of suicides into a river; people in Dahomey threw them where they would become carrion. As often as cultural groups made suicide taboo, however, others respected it or even revered it. In North America the Zuni frowned on it, but the Navajo and the Hopi did not; in the Pacific suicide was condemned in the Andaman Islands, but praised in the Fijis.

The Bible never condemned suicide, although in later times the rabbinical Talmud did and the Christian church followed suit. Samson, Saul, Abimilech, Achitophel—their stories are told without censure. The term *suicide* itself only appeared in the seventeenth century. Not until the sixth century was the act proscribed; until that time, in the absence of biblical authority, condemnation of suicide had to be inferred from the sixth of the Ten Commandments, "Thou shalt not kill."

The Greeks were more judicious and therefore more selectively in favor of suicide than the Jews, and so were the Romans. Both the Stoics and the Epicureans approved it in principle. Zeno approved and so did Cleanthes. Seneca actually committed suicide, to forestall the murderous Nero's fun and games, and his wife Paulina joined him. On the other hand, the Pythagoreans, opponents of Hippocratic medicine, having their special knowledge of the god's decrees, opposed suicide because of what Islam later called kismet. (After all, if one "knows" what a transcendental and ultimate will forbids, one would be prudent not to do it.)

Plato allowed euthanasia, as Aristotle did, but in the manner of suicide, not in the manner of "letting a patient go." Homer and Euripides thought well of Jocasta committing suicide after she learned that her new husband Oedipus was her own son—which was, perhaps, an excessive and irrational reaction, but humanly understandable because of the strength of the incest taboo. The Romans, as we all know, allowed the *libertas mori* for a great many reasons; they denied it only to criminals, soldiers, and slaves—for obvious military and economic reasons. Justinian's *Digest* spelled out the subject judiciously.

Christian Europe started moving from pagan Rome's compassionate regard for the dignity of free persons to the savagery of an indiscriminating condemnation of all suicide in the Middle Ages only after the Greco-Roman civilization had been ended by the Barbarian-Teutonic hordes. Once the classical philosophy was buried, the Catholic-medieval synthesis was able to take over, and one of its first major elements was an absolute taboo on suicide. In the manorial system nearly everybody was enfeoffed to somebody else; hence suicide was, in effect, a soldier's or a slave's unlawful escape from somebody's possession. It was fundamentally "subversive" of property rights.

The Christian moralists never put it that way, of course. Instead, they said that human life is a divine monopoly: "Our lives are God's." To take one's own life, therefore, is to invade Jesus Christ's property rights because he has saved us "and we are therefore his." This mystical theology was the bottom layer of the moral and canonical prohibition. It led some theologians to say that Judas Iscariot's suicide in remorse and despair was even more wicked than his earlier betrayal of Jesus and Jesus' consequent crucifixion.

A FALSE TURNING POINT

St. Augustine marked the turning point in the hardening process. He was the first to make the prohibition absolute. None of the later anti-suicide moralists improved on him; even Aquinas added only "It is unnatural," thus buttressing the theology with a religious metaphysics of "natural law."

We can outline Augustine's objections to any and all suicide in four propositions: (1) If we are innocent, we may not kill the innocent; if we are guilty, we may not take justice into our own hands. (2) The sixth commandment of the Decalogue forbids it, *non occides;* suicide is homicide; it is a felony, *felo de se.* (3) Our duty is to bear suffering with fortitude; to escape is to evade our role as soldiers of Christ. (4) Suicide is the worst sin; it precludes repentance; to do it in a state of grace (after one is saved, or cleansed of sin by Christ's blood) means one dies out of grace (unsaved, eternally lost or rejected). Augustine allowed an occasional exception for martyrs who had God's express directive or "guidance" to kill themselves; they were said to be acting as innocently as those who sin *ex ignorantia inculcata* (in invincible ignorance). This is the argument Augustine used to answer the Donatists, a Christian sect that pointed out that dying baptized in a state of grace, by one's own hand, was better than living long enough to fall back into sin, losing one's chance to have eternal life in heaven.

At the end of the Holy Roman hegemony, people began to reason again. By 1561 Thomas More (the "man for all seasons" who died for conscience's sake) had allowed suicide in his *Utopia,* even though Sir Thomas Browne frowned on it in his *Religio Medici* (1642). Montaigne backed More, and so it went. The great classic *coup de grâce* to the moral prohibition of suicide came with David Hume's essay *On Suicide* (1777), in which he reasoned that if suicide is wrong it must be because it offends God, one's neighbor, or one's self, and then showed how this would not always be true. Hume was joined by Voltaire, Rousseau, Montesquieu, and d'Holbach.

The conventional wisdom after nearly a thousand years of prohibition continued unchanged, as attempted suicides were hanged from the public gibbet. In Christian France, as in animist Dahomey, the bodies of the executed were thrown on garbage dumps. The properties of suicides were confiscated in England until 1870, and prison was the legal penalty for attempts until 1961.

At last, in the Suicide Act of 1961, England stopped making it a crime for a person, whether well or ill, to end his life or attempt to do so. There are only a few places left in the world where the courts are still trying to catch up to that kind of moral "sanity." Courts of law today are seldom as unethical about suicide as the conventional moralists continue to be.

Always and everywhere we find cultural variety and difference all along the spectrum of ethical opinion—from blanket prohibition to selective justification. In a very sane and discriminating fashion most communities, both savage and civilized, have believed that disposing of one's own life is like disposing of one's own property, that is, a personal election.

It is on this last ground that most governments in the West have been opposed to suicide. They have followed Aristotle and Plato, who contended pragmatically that except for grave reasons suicide seriously deprived the community of soldiers to defend it and workers to do its labor of head and hand. How weighty this objection is now, in an age of overpopulation, cybernated warfare, and automated industry, is an open question. In any case, the "right" to die is not right if and when it invades the well-being of others. On the other hand, when it is truly and only a personal choice, it is right. To deny this is to deny the integrity of persons, to reduce them to being only functions or appendages of systems of lords and seigneurs, or church and state.

TYPES OF SUICIDE

Just as facts cannot tell us which things to value (although they may help) or how to rank them as priorities, neither can typologies. This caution applies, for example, to Emile Durkheim's famous classification of suicides into egoistic and altruistic, which is close to what we have come to mean in more recent days by "inner directed" and "other directed"—in the language of Riesman's *Lonely Crowd.*

Strong self-sustaining personalities are able (have the "ego strength") to defy cultural disapproval when or if a balance of pro-life and pro-death factors seems to weigh against going on living. As Albert Camus said, "Judging whether life is or is not worth living amounts to answering the fundamental question of philosophy." To drive home his point that philosophy is not merely impersonal abstraction, he added drily, "I have never seen anyone die for the ontological argument." There are times, although we may hope not often, when people find that the flame is no longer worth the candle. History and literature abound with instances.

Similarly, on the altruistic side, there are times when sacrificial love and loyalty may call on us for a tragic decision, to choose death for the sake of a wider good than self. The decision is made pragmatically, to promote the greater good or the lesser evil. An example is Captain Oates in the Antarctic snafu, who eliminated himself to speed up the escape of his companions; other instances are disabled grandparents pushing off on ice floes to relieve hungry Eskimos and brave men staying on the sinking *Titanic* or dropping off from overloaded lifeboats.

Durkheim had a third type of suicides, the anomic—those who suffer anomie, who have come to despair for either subjective reasons (including psychogenic illness) or objective reasons (maybe unemployability or outright social rejection). They reach a point where they cannot "care less." Demoralized, unnerved, disoriented, they throw in their remaining chips. One recalls Jeb Magruder telling the Senate Watergate committee, by way of self-excuse, that he had lost his "ethical compass." Suicide out of anomie or being normless, just as in cases when it is done out of ego strength or for loyalty reasons, may be rationally well-founded and prudent or may not. Suicides of all kinds, in any typology, can be wise or foolish.

This is perhaps the point at which to challenge directly and flatly the widespread assumption that "suicides are sick people, out of their gourds." This canard has lodged itself deeply even in the mental attitudes of physicians. It has managed to become the "conventional wisdom" of psychiatric medicine, partly, no doubt, because psychiatrists deal so much with false suicides whose verbal or nonverbal threats or "attempts" are signals of emotional or mental distress. Nevertheless, for all its persistence, the idea is basically silly.

Like universalized or absolutized moral norms, this one, too, is undiscriminating—a frequent diagnosis turned into a universalized stereotype. Some suicides are suffering from what Freud first called misplaced aggression and later thought to be diseased superego, but not all are. To say *all* is to be playing with universalized characterizations, and universals of any kind are fantasies, not empirical realites. (The hypocrisy of the courts has done a lot to encourage the dogma that suicides are unhinged.) The fact is that suicide sometimes can be psychiatrically discredited or sometimes can be ethically approved, depending on the case.

Those suicides who tell us about the fears and doubts that go through their minds are the "attempteds," not the successful and thorough ones, and the result is a marked bias or skew to the speculations and theories of therapists. Even more speculative are the ideas of writers who have lively imaginations (Thomas Mann, Boris Pasternak), especially when imagination is combined with a grasp of psychological jargon. Real suicides rarely leave any record and even more rarely explain themselves in any reflective detail; there are only a few exceptions like Arthur Schopenhauer, who thought suicide through but did not do it, and Sylvia Plath, who did. We only have to read Lael Wertenbaker's *Death of a Man* (1957), the story of her husband's noble and sane decision to cheat Big C, to get a more realistic appreciation of what suicide can be.

SUICIDE TODAY

In recent years the ethical issue about human initiatives in death and dying has been posed most poignantly for the common run of those in medical care, in the treatment of the terminally ill. Resuscitative techniques now compel them to decide when to stop preserving and supporting life; people no longer just die. What is called negative euthanasia, letting the patient die without any further struggle against it, is a daily event in hospitals. About 200,000 legally unenforceable "living wills" have been recorded, appealing to doctors, families, pastors, and lawyers to stop treatment at some balance point of pro-life, pro-death assessment.

What is called positive euthanasia—doing something to shorten or end life deliberately—is the form in which suicide is the question—as a voluntary, direct choice of death.

For a long time the Christian moralists have distinguished between negative or indirectly willed suicide, like not taking a place in one of the *Titanic*'s lifeboats, and positive or directly willed suicide, like jumping out of a lifeboat to make room for a fellow victim of a shipwreck. The moralists mean that we may choose to allow an evil by acts of omission but not to do an evil by acts of commission. The moralists contend that since all suicide is evil we may only "allow" it; we may not "do" it. The moralists do not mean that death is evil, only that dying is evil if it is done freely and directly by personal choice. Choosing to die is self-murder, just as a physician or friend helping you die at your earnest request would be guilty of murder.

Is it not ridiculous, however, to say that given the desirability of escape from this mortal coil or a tragic "crunch" in which one elects to give one's life for another value, all acts of omission to that end are licit, yet all acts of commission to the same end are wrong? Taboo thinking such as "all suicide is wrong" enlists false reasoning and invites inhumane consequences. The end or goal or purpose in both direct (positive) and indirect (negative) euthanasia is precisely the same—the end of the patient's life, release from pointless misery and dehumanizing loss of functions. The logic here is inexorable.

As Kant said, if we will the end we will the means, and if the means required is inordinate or disproportionate we give up the end. The old maxim of some religious thinkers was *finis sanctificat media*. Human acts of any kind, including suicide, depend for their ethical status on the proportion of good between the end sought and the means needed to accomplish it. Only if the means were inappropriate or too costly would the end have to be foregone. It follows that suicide is probably sometimes a fitting act and well worth doing.

How can it be right for a person to go over the cliff's edge helplessly blindfolded, while we stand by doing nothing to prevent it, but wrong if that person removes the blindfold and steps off with eyes open? It is naïve or obtuse to contend that if we choose to die slowly, forlornly, willy-nilly, by a natural disintegration from something like cancer or starvation, we have no complicity in our death and the death is not suicide; but if we deliberately our "quietus make with a bare bodkin," it is suicide. Every person's fight with death is lost before it begins. What makes the struggle worthwhile, therefore, cannot lie in the outcome. It lies in the dignity with which the fight is waged and the way it finds an end.

The summary principle is limpid clear: Not to do anything is a decision to act every bit as much as deciding to *do* what we would accomplish by "not" acting.

Consideration of suicide for social reasons (Durkheim's altruistic type) can easily lead to a philosophical debate about ethical egoism or self-interest *versus* social integration and utilitarian concern for the greatest good of the greatest number. Whether we limit our obligation to others to the parameters of enlightened self-interest or, more altruistically, of social solidarism, it still follows that we may be called to suicide for heroic or for sacrificial reasons. The fact that sometimes suicide subjects are unconsciously wanting to die anyway (Menninger, 1938) is psychiatrically important but ethically irrelevant—unless, of course, we slide into the semantic swamp and assert that all who sacrifice their lives—parents, soldiers, police officers, researchers, explorers, or whoever—are sick.

More problematic and subtle than suicide for medical or social reasons are what we may call the personal cases. The ethical principle here is the integrity of persons and respect for their freedom. Sometimes suicides act for profoundly personal, deeply private reasons. Often enough other people, even those close to the suicides, cannot add things up in the same way to justify the election of death. If there is no clear and countervailing injustice involved, however, surely the values of self-determination and liberty weigh in the suicide's favor. Social, physical, esthetic, and mental deficiencies, when combined, could weigh against the worth of a person's life. And who is to be the accountant or assessor if not the one whose death it is?

CONCLUSION

It appears that a basic issue is whether quality of life is more valuable than life *qua* life. And defense of suicide has to opt for quality, not quantity. The sacralists, those who invest life with a sacred entelechy of some kind, consequently make all direct control over life taboo. (We see this in the abortion debate as well as in the question of suicide.)

This question, whether we may act on a quality-of-life ethic or must go on with the medieval sanctity-of-life ethic, runs through nearly every problem in the field of biomedical policy—genetics, transplants, the determination of death, allocation of scarce treatment resources, management of the dying patient, human experimentation, fetal research, nearly everything.

Quality concern requires us to reorder values; those who promptly and dogmatically put being alive as the first-order value need to reappraise their ethics. One's life is a value to be perceived in relation to other values. At best it is only *primus inter pares*. Without life other things are of no value to us, but by the same token without other things life may be of no value to us. In *The Tyranny of Survival* Daniel Callahan puts it succinctly: "Unlike other animals, human beings are consciously able to kill themselves by suicide; some people choose to die." They want more than "mere survival," he thinks. "Models which work with ants do not work well when extrapolated to human beings."

The reason for this, we can add, is that human beings, unlike purely instinctual creatures, do not regard life as an end in itself. Life, to be up to human standards, has to integrate a number of other values to make it worth our while. Human beings can choose to die not only for reasons of love and loyalty but just because life happens to be too sour or bare. In Sean O'Casey's words, a time may come when laughter is no longer a weapon against evil.

The ethical problem, how to make value choices, comes down, as we have seen, to whether we reason with or without absolutes of right and wrong. Bayet back in 1922 had his own way of putting it in *Le Suicide et la Morale*. He said there are two kinds of approaches: an ethic of a priori rules and taboos or universal prohibitions or, alternatively, a *"morale nuancée,"* an ethic rooted in variables and discrimination, that judges acts by their consequences, a posteriori. This essay is built on moral nuances.

Socrates and Karl Jaspers, 2,300 years apart, thought that the business of philosophy is to prepare us for death. Religionists, in their own way, have taken hold of that task; they have coped by a denial maneuver and a counterassertion of eternal life. Philosophers have ignored the problem for the most part. A good start was made with Epictetus' dictum: "When I am, death is not. When death is, I am not. Therefore we can never have anything to do with death. Why fear it?" Or take, in present-day terms, Camus' opening remark in his absurd essay *The Myth of Sisyphus,* that there is "but one truly serious philosophical problem, and that is suicide."

We have a striking paradigm for the ethics of suicide. In his *Note-*

books 1914–16 Wittgenstein says that suicide is the "elementary sin"—blandly assuming, in tyro fashion, that survival is the highest good, even though it is individually impossible and corporately improbable that experience will bear this assumption out. Only on that unacknowledged premise was he able to say that "if anything is not allowed then suicide is not allowed." But then his superb mind forced him to ask, in conclusion, "Or is even suicide in itself neither good nor evil?" There, in a phrase, is the whole point ethically. Nothing in itself is either good or evil, neither life nor death. Quality is always extrinsic and contingent.

The full circle is being drawn. In classical times suicide was a tragic option, for human dignity's sake. Then for centuries it was a sin. Then it became a crime. Then a sickness. Soon it will become a choice again. Suicide is the signature of freedom.

Part Two
When Do We Call It Suicide?

7

Suicide, Self-Sacrifice, and Coercion

William E. Tolhurst

That not all self-caused deaths are suicides is obvious, but what is not so clear is how the line should be drawn to distinguish those which are from those which are not. In many cases the difficulty in determining whether a self-caused death is suicide does not stem from a lack of empirical evidence but rather from the lack of a clear account of what makes a particular self-caused death a case of suicide. It is the aim of this paper to provide and defend a definition of suicide which will clarify what is at issue in these cases. In the process I shall consider the relevance of altruistic motivation and of coercion to the determination of whether a person has committed suicide.

After a brief discussion of the relevance of particular cases to the assessment of possible definitions, I shall begin by showing that any definition, such as Durkheim's or Brandt's, which implies that the mere foreknowledge that one's death will result from one's actions is a sufficient condition for suicide must be rejected. Then I shall go on to consider what, in addition to this foreknowledge, is required if a self-caused death is to be properly classed as a suicide. The definitions offered by Margolis

From *The Southern Journal of Philosophy* 21 (1983): 109–121. Reprinted by permission of the publisher.

and Beauchamp will be examined, and it will be argued that they are inadequate and that the absence of altruistic motivation and coercion are not necessary conditions for a person's death to be a suicide. Having shown that these alternatives should be rejected, I shall defend the view that suicide is a matter of successfully implementing a course of action in order to bring about one's death.

Any attempt to provide a definition for a term in a natural language must take as its basis the linguistic intuitions of native speakers about the proper application of this term to particular cases, both actual and possible. With respect to the concept of suicide, there are three relevant categories of cases: (1) clear cases of suicide, (2) clear cases of self-caused deaths which are not suicides, and (3) cases of self-caused deaths where our pretheoretical dispositions to apply or withhold the label do not provide us with a clear verdict. Of course, the boundaries of these categories will inevitably be imprecise. The most one can hope for is a definition which yields the correct results in those cases on which all or most native speakers agree and plausible results in all the others. In what follows, I shall argue that the definition of suicide as successfully implementing a course of action in order to bring about one's death meets this criterion better than any of the alternative definitions defended in the literature thus far.

One further working assumption should be noted at this point. I shall assume that the concept of suicide is not morally loaded in the way that the concept of murder is, that it is not part of the meaning of the term 'suicide' that suicide is morally objectionable. I take it that the concept of murder is such that a homicide could not properly be termed a murder unless it was, in some sense, wrong (either legally or morally). The case is different with the concept of suicide. One can sensibly ask whether suicide is ever morally permissible and while those who would answer in the affirmative might turn out to be in error, they do not contradict themselves. Thus the question of which self-caused deaths are morally objectionable is distinct from the question of which self-caused deaths are suicide.

I. SUICIDE AND FOREKNOWLEDGE

Clearly those who cause their own deaths while ignorant of the likelihood that their actions will have this result should not be considered suicides.

Thus the foreknowledge that a course of action upon which one has embarked is likely to bring about one's death is at least a necessary condition for a self-caused death to be a suicide. Some proposed definitions of suicide, most notably those of Durkheim[1] and Brandt,[2] take this condition to be not only necessary but also sufficient. Durkheim held that "the term suicide is applied to all cases of death resulting directly or indirectly from a positive or negative act of the victim himself which he knows will produce this result."[3] Brandt's definition though worded differently also implies that the foreknowledge that a person's death will result from his action is sufficient to make that person's death a suicide.

"Suicide" is conveniently defined, for our purposes, as doing something which results in one's death, either from the intention of ending one's life or the intention to bring about some other state of affairs (such as relief from pain) which one thinks it certain or highly probable can be achieved only by means of death or will produce death.[4]

That these views are mistaken can be demonstrated by the following hypothetical example which I take to be a clear case of a self-caused death which is not a suicide (i.e. a case of type [2]). Imagine the following. A doctor with a defective heart knows that she will die soon unless she has a transplant. Let us suppose further that she has a patient whose heart would be an ideal candidate for a transplant and that she can kill her patient while making it appear that the patient died of natural causes. If our imaginary doctor were to reject this option because it would require her to murder her patient, and if this condition were sufficient, then we would have to say that in so deciding the doctor has committed suicide (on the assumption that her death results from the decision). But clearly our imaginary doctor would not, in any ordinary sense of the term, be committing suicide in refusing to murder her patient. Thus Durkheim's and Brandt's definitions must be rejected.

Since this condition is necessary but not sufficient, the question that remains is what additional restrictions must be added to rule out cases of the sort described above. Two prominent features of our imaginary case present themselves as bases for possible restrictions. One is that our imaginary doctor's death is the result of what Durkheim would call a negative act of the victim, i.e., it results from her decision not to do something. The other is that the doctor does not choose the option which results in her death for selfish reasons. Presumably it is her concern for the welfare of her patient which motivates her decision. A brief argument is sufficient to show the irrelevance of the first consideration, but the second will be considered at some length in the next section.

One might argue for the first condition on the grounds that suicide is essentially a matter of killing oneself and that one whose death results from a negative act or an omission to do something has not killed himself and hence cannot have committed suicide. That this consideration, although initially plausible, is ultimately irrelevant can be shown by the fact that it is clearly possible for a person to commit suicide by willfully deciding not to perform an action which is necessary to sustain his life. For example, imagine a man who finds himself in need of a routine (relatively safe and painless) operation which is necessary to save his life. Suppose further that this man has no abnormal fear of operations, but rather that he finds his present and foreseeable future life not worth living; it is characterized by a high level of psychic and/or physical suffering which is unrelated to the condition which necessitates the operation. If this person were to refuse to have the operation because he wanted to end it all, his subsequent demise would properly be classed as suicide. I take it that this case falls into category (1) as a clear case of suicide. Thus I conclude that it is, in principle, possible for the category of suicide to include what we might call cases of passive suicide[5] where a person intentionally allows himself to die.

2. SUICIDE AND SELF-SACRIFICE

Margolis has argued[6] that altruistically motivated suicides are not possible. His reasons for this are both clear and mistaken. Margolis takes suicide to be essentially a matter of choosing death for its own sake. In the case of genuine suicide, according to Margolis, the victim's "overriding concern is to end his own life. . . ." Those who bring about their own deaths in order to benefit others are not willing their deaths as an ultimate goal of their actions; therefore, they fail to meet his definition of suicide. However, Margolis's definition of suicide is clearly mistaken; almost no one who commits suicide (in the ordinary sense of the term) could meet the conditions of his definition. A great many suicides are the result of the victim's desire to end his suffering (psychic or physical) and in none of these cases is death chosen for its own sake.

But even if Margolis's definition is mistaken, it might still be the case that altruistic motivation is incompatible with suicide. Certainly, it is possible to imagine a great many altruistically motivated self-caused deaths which are not suicides. The following are representative examples.

Case A: The pilot of a disabled plane decides not to use her parachute and to remain in the plane in order to prevent it from crashing in a populated area.

Case B: One of the occupants of an overloaded lifeboat decides to go overboard in order to prevent the boat from sinking.

Case C: A soldier covers a live hand grenade with his body in order to protect his comrades.

Such cases are quite often discussed in the literature and do pose a difficult problem for anyone who would seek to provide a plausible definition of suicide. I take it that these are clear cases of nonsuicidal self-caused death and that an adequate definition should exclude them. But from this it does not follow that all altruistically motivated self-caused deaths should be excluded. That is, the feature of these cases which is responsible for their not being cases of suicide might turn out to have nothing to do with the fact that they are cases of self-sacrifice.

That this is so is supported by the existence of other cases of sacrificial self-caused deaths which do seem to be suicides. One such case (which Margolis discusses) is that of the Buddhist monk who burns himself to death to express his opposition to a war. This seems to me to be a reasonably clear case of suicide, but since Margolis disagrees I shall appeal to another in support of my contention that altruistic motivation is compatible with suicide. Imagine a person who has discovered that he is terminally ill. Since his family is in dire need of money and his life insurance policy contains a double-indemnity clause he arranges a fatal "accident" to benefit his family. I take it that one does not have to be an insurance investigator to see that this is a clear case of suicide. Thus I conclude that altruistically motivated suicides are, in principle, possible and that while an adequate definition should exclude cases A-C, it should not imply that an absence of altruistic motivation is a necessary condition for suicide. The failure of this criterion leaves the question as to why our conscientious doctor is not a suicide unanswered. In the next section I shall consider Beauchamp's attempt to answer this question and with it his contention that coercion is incompatible with suicide.

3. SUICIDE AND COERCION

If the reason our imaginary doctor does not commit suicide in refusing to murder her patient is not because she merely lets her death happen nor because she acts out of concern for others, one might well wonder what it is about this case that makes it a nonsuicide. To this question Beauchamp gives the following answer. The doctor is not a suicide because "the condition causing death is not brought about by the agent for the purpose of ending his or her life."[7] However, Beauchamp does not hold that this condition is the only one which must be added to come up with a plausible definition since he holds that a self-caused death may fail to be a suicide if the agent acted under coercion. His candidate for a definition is as follows:

> An act is a suicide if a person intentionally brings about his or her own death in circumstances where others do not coerce him or her to the action, except in those cases where death is caused by conditions not specifically arranged by the agent for the purpose of bringing about his or her own death.[8]

Although this might seem to be a preferable alternative, it, too, must be rejected. The reason is that neither the absence of coercion nor the condition that the agent's death not be caused by conditions not arranged by him in order to cause his death are necessary conditions for committing suicide.

That the latter condition is not necessary can be shown by the following case. A man has decided that his life is no longer worth living and proposes to end it all by jumping into a nearby ravine. However, on the way to the ravine he finds himself about to be engulfed by an avalanche which he could avoid without much difficulty. Nonetheless he allows himself to be killed by the avalanche and thus saves the trouble of walking to the ravine. Surely this man has committed suicide even though he was killed by conditions which he did not arrange in order to bring about his death. Thus this requirement must be rejected as too strong. However, if we merely delete it from Beauchamp's definition, then it will succumb to the case of our conscientious doctor.

Although Beauchamp does not offer any arguments for his contention that coercion is incompatible with suicide (he seems to think that it is too obvious to need support), he does provide two illustrative cases.

Consider . . . a captured soldier who, given the "choice" of being executed or of executing himself, chooses self-execution. Since coercion is heavily involved in this intentional self-killing, we do not classify it as a suicide, just as we do not think that Socrates committed suicide by intentionally drinking the hemlock, thereby causing his death.[9]

Both the contention and the cases are problematic. It is by no means clear that these are not cases of suicide; at best they seem to fall into category (3) as cases where the pre-theoretical dispositions of native speakers to apply the term do not provide a clear verdict. Indeed, R. G. Frey has recently argued that Socrates did commit suicide.[10] While his argument may be mistaken, the fact that he is prepared to offer one for this conclusion is some indication that the issue is open to doubt and that this case should not be cited without argument as a clear example of nonsuicide. Furthermore, even if one were to agree that Socrates' self-caused death is not a suicide, one might well wonder whether it is the presence of coercion which accounts for this fact, if it be a fact. This is because one might well hold that Socrates drank the hemlock freely. Certainly Socrates had ample opportunity to escape execution, but he freely chose to stay.

In the absence of any clear reasons for thinking that suicide is incompatible with coercion, let us consider some reasons for thinking that it is not. Japanese literature abounds with stories of samurai who are pressured into committing *seppuku*, ritual disembowelment. For example, the historical events upon which the play *Chushingura* is based involve a vendetta which was instigated by the forced *seppuku* of Lord Asano Naganori of Akō and whose perpetrators (forty-six *rōnin*) were punished by being condemned to commit *seppuku*. It seems plausible to suppose that anyone who commits *seppuku* commits suicide. Since people can be (and have been) forced to commit *seppuku*, it is reasonable to conclude that coerced suicide is possible. Thus Donald Keene describes one of the events which set off the vendetta mentioned above as follows: ". . . Tsunayoshi, the shogun, was so outraged by this unseemly breach of decorum in the palace that he commanded Asano to commit suicide."[11]

The view that coercion is compatible with suicide is further supported by a consideration of the following hypothetical cases.

Case D: Smith has discovered that he has terminal cancer. In order to avoid a long and painful death, he shoots himself.

Case E: Jones is a soldier and is about to be captured by the enemy. He knows if he is captured, he will be tortured to death. In order to avoid a long and painful death, he shoots himself.

Case F: Brown is a prisoner of a sadistic tyrant who informs him that he can either kill himself or be tortured to death. (The tyrant would marginally prefer the latter option, but for reasons unknown to me is willing to allow Brown a choice.) In order to avoid a long and painful death, he shoots himself.

Case G: Robinson is a prisoner of a tyrant who wants him to kill himself and who informs Robinson that unless he does so he will be tortured to death. In order to avoid a long and painful death, he shoots himself.

Although the circumstances surrounding the actions of Smith, Jones, Brown, and Robinson are markedly different, each is faced with substantially the same choice. Furthermore, each is equally free (or unfree) to choose between the options available to him even though these are, given the circumstances, severely limited. However, only case G clearly involves a person who has been coerced into killing himself.[12] I take it that Smith and Jones have clearly committed suicide and since Brown and Robinson have the same options as Smith and Jones and acted for the same reasons, I conclude that it is reasonable to suppose that Brown and Robinson have committed suicide as well. Thus I conclude that suicide is compatible with coercion.

At this point some discussion of why people might be misled into thinking that altruistic motivation and coercion are incompatible with suicide may well be in order. One explanation may be the simple fact that the most common cases of suicide do not involve these factors and hence these sorts of cases are easily overlooked. In addition to this, the presence of altruistic motivation and of coercion in a case of self-killing has a marked affect on its moral status. Altruistic acts tend to be morally admirable and those who act under coercion are less blameworthy for their actions than they would have been had coercion not been present. Many people are inclined to view suicide as selfish and blameworthy and when confronted with self-killings that are neither may be tempted to deny that these self-killings are suicide. However, in my view the proper response to these cases should be to reconsider the moral status of suicide. It seems clear that suicide is not selfish and blameworthy by definition and hence these essentially moral considerations ought not to distort the classification of self-caused deaths as suicides and nonsuicides.

4. SUICIDE DEFINED

In this section I propose to defend the view that a person has committed suicide if and only if that person has brought about his death intentionally.[13] In defending this answer it will be necessary to consider in some detail the question of what makes an action intentional. It will also be necessary to distinguish two senses in which an action might be said to be intentional, a strong and a weak sense. The analysis of suicide will require a self-caused death to be intentional in the strong sense. In explicating this sense of intentional action I shall assume the basic correctness of the causal account of intentional action advocated by Goldman and others.[14] The main idea of this account is that an intentional action is one which has the right sort of causal history, roughly one which is caused by the agent's beliefs and desires in the right way.

In order to distinguish the weak from the strong sense of intentional action it is useful to begin with an imaginary example. A person, let's call her Mary, has decided to buy a Coke in order to quench her thirst and has proceeded to put the requisite amount of money in the nearest Coke machine. In the process she has (a) moved her arm, (b) put the money in the machine, (c) obtained a Coke, (d) increased the profits of the owners of the machine, and (e) emptied the machine of Coca-Cola.[15] Let us suppose further Mary knew that (b) would result in the increase in profits but not that it would empty the machine. We may also suppose that Mary had no desire to bring about the increase in profits but that she was willing to accept this consequence as a necessary concomitant of the optimal way of getting a Coke. In this case (a), (b), and (c) are both strongly and weakly intentional; (e) is neither; and (d) is weakly but not strongly intentional.

In explaining the difference between strongly and weakly intentional action it will be convenient to use Goldman's notion of act-generation. Sometimes two actions are related in such a way that it is appropriate to say that the agent performed one by performing the other. With regard to the above example, one can say that by putting the money in the machine Mary performed (c), (d), and (e). To say that one act, a, has generated another act, a*, is just to say that the agent performed a* by performing a.[16]

It is clear why one would want to hold that (c) is intentional; (c) is an action which Mary wanted to perform and (we may suppose) her successful performance of it resulted from her desire to perform it and her beliefs about how she might perform it by means of an appropriate causal chain. It is also apparent why (a) and (b) are intentional as well since both resulted in the proper way from Mary's desire to perform (c) together with her belief that (b) would generate (c) and that (a) would generate (b). This suggests the following (strong) sense of intentional action:

> An act, a, is strongly intentional iff [if and only if] (1) there is an act, b, which the agent wanted to perform and a either is or generates b and (2) the agent's performance of a is caused in an appropriate manner by the agent's desire to perform b together with his beliefs about how b might be generated.[17]

Clearly, (a), (b), and (c) are strongly intentional while (d) and (e) are not because Mary had no desire to perform (d) or (e) and neither generated any action which she wanted to perform.

But despite the fact that neither (d) nor (e) is strongly intentional there is an important difference between them. For one thing, Mary could be held responsible for performing (d) but not for performing (e). Mary's performance of (d) as a result of performing (b) was foreseen and hence it was not accidental in the way that (e) was. Thus one might hold (d) but not (e) to be intentional because Mary knew that it would be generated by an act which would generate the action which she wanted to perform. The weaker sense of intentional action can be expressed as follows:

> An act, a, is weakly intentional if and only if (1) there is an act, b, which the agent wanted to perform and a is generated in the process of performing b; (2) the agent believed that a would be generated in the process of performing b; and (3) the agent's performance of a results in an appropriate manner from his desire to perform b together with his beliefs about how b might be generated.

Being weakly intentional is thus necessary but not sufficient for being strongly intentional. Actions which are weakly but not strongly intentional usually involve the causation of effects which are, to use the scholastic terminology, foreseen but unintended. Thus something like the above distinction seems to be presupposed by the doctrine of double effect. One advantage of this analysis is that it provides a clear explanation of why those who hold that it is always wrong to perform an action which has the death of an innocent person as a foreseen and intended consequence would judge suicide to be morally impermissible. This is because an agent's self-caused death will be strongly intentional only if the agent directly intended his death.

In defending the contention that suicide consists in an agent's bringing about his own death in such a way that this action is strongly intentional, it will be useful to reconsider some of the problem cases discussed above. The first of these concerned the relationship between foreknowledge and suicide. The case of the conscientious doctor demonstrates that the foreknowledge that an agent's death will result from his action is not sufficient to render that agent's death a suicide. When an agent performs an action, a, which has a consequence, c, the agent has performed the action of bringing about c by performing a. If, furthermore, the agent realized that c would result from a (and c did result from a in an appropriate way), then the agent's action of bringing it about that c is weakly intentional. This being so, it seems clear that since our imaginary doctor knew that her death would result from her act of refusing to murder her patient, her death is weakly intentional. However, from this it does not follow that it is strongly intentional. If we assume that the doctor did not want to die, then her action of bringing about her death, which is generated by her refusal to murder her patient, is strongly intentional only if there is some other action which she wanted to perform and which is generated by her action of bringing about her death. Since we may assume that there is no such action her action of bringing about her death is not strongly intentional and the definition implies, rightly, that her death is not a suicide.

The second problem considered above concerned the relationship between suicide and self-sacrifice. In most cases altruistically motivated self-caused deaths are not strongly intended. This is true not only of the conscientious doctor but also of cases A, B, and C described above. In all of these cases the agent did not want to die and there is no action generated by the agent's action of bringing about his death which the agent wanted to perform. Thus these deaths are not strongly intended and the definition implies that they are not suicides. Nonetheless the person who arranges a fatal "accident" so that his family can collect more insurance money is correctly classed as a suicide by this definition. In this case there is an action which the agent wanted to perform, i.e., bringing it about that his family collects twice as much money, which is generated by the action of causing his death. This being so, his death is strongly intended and the definition implies that it is a suicide.

The third problem concerned cases of passive suicide where a person refuses to avoid life-threatening conditions in order to end his life. In these cases the agent wants to die and brings about his death by his refusal. Since the action of bringing about his death is an action the agent wants to perform, it is strongly intentional in these cases, and the definition implies that these deaths are suicides as well. Thus I conclude that the analysis has plausible implications for the problem cases discussed above. Having disposed of these cases, I will now consider the somewhat more difficult question of whether or not Socrates' self-caused death is a case of suicide.

It is clear that if this definition is correct, then our ability to decide in any given case whether a self-caused death is a suicide will depend on our ability to ascertain the agent's beliefs and desires. With regard to Socrates we may assume that Socrates wanted to comply with Athenian law and that he believed that his action of drinking the hemlock would generate the action of complying with Athenian law. We may also suppose that Socrates knew that his action of drinking the hemlock would cause his death. However, these assumptions by themselves do not enable us to determine whether Socrates committed suicide. In order to do this we need to know what Socrates believed about the relations between the following actions: (a) drinking the hemlock, (b) causing Socrates' death, and (c) complying with Athenian law. We are assuming that Socrates believed that (a) would generate (b) and (c) and that Socrates wanted to perform (c). From this it follows that (a) and (c) are strongly intentional and that (b) is (at least) weakly intentional. The crucial question is whether Socrates believed that the law required him merely to drink the hemlock or whether he believed that the law required him to bring about his death. If Socrates believed the former then he believed that (a) would generate (c) directly and that (c) would not be generated by (b). If this was the case then Socrates' death was weakly but not strongly intentional and he did not commit suicide. However, if Socrates believed that the performance of (b) was necessary to generate (c), that (a) would generate (c) by means of generating (b), then (b) was strongly intentional and Socrates' death was a suicide. Given the difficulty in determining Socrates' act-generational beliefs, i.e., in determining his action-plan, in such fine detail, it is clear why the question of whether his death was a suicide is controversial. Since the aim of this discussion is merely to illustrate how the proposed analysis applies to problem cases of this sort, I shall not speculate on which of the two hypotheses concerning Socrates' act-generational beliefs is the more plausible. Although this and other cases are problematic because of our difficulties in ascertaining the agent's beliefs, there is another class of intractable cases to be considered whose problematic character arises from a very different source which will provide the subject for the following section. These arise out of the difficulties involved in specifying the sort of causal connection which must obtain between an agent's beliefs and desires and his actions if these are to be intentional (in either sense).

5. THE PROBLEM OF DEVIANT CAUSAL CHAINS

In sketching out the definitions of both strongly and weakly intentional action it was necessary to use the vague requirements that the causal link between the agent's beliefs and desires be of the right sort. Although the vagueness of this requirement is not a barrier to understanding the difference between these two different types of intentional action, it is clear that a fully adequate account of intentional action must replace it with a more informative description of the appropriate sort of causal chain. This project is one which has proved troublesome not only for the causal theory of action but also for causal theories of reference, knowledge, and perception. Although the resolution of this difficulty is clearly beyond the scope of this paper, it merits some disussion in this context. In particular, a discussion of it will show both how and why the determination of whether certain kinds of self-caused deaths are suicides depends upon a more detailed account of intentional action.

It will be useful to begin with a clear example of a self-caused death in which the agent has failed to commit suicide not because he failed to have the right beliefs and desires but because the causal link between his beliefs and desires was not of the right sort. Suppose that a person has decided to commit suicide by throwing himself in front of a truck, but that just after he throws himself in front of the nearest one (and before he is hit by it) he is killed by a stray bullet from a shootout between two street gangs which just happens to be in progress nearby. Thus he is already dead by the time he is hit by the truck. Although this person has tried to commit suicide, his premature death prevented him from succeeding. It is clear in this case that despite the person's intention to commit suicide and the fact that his beliefs and desires led to his performing an action which caused his death, the person's death is an accident and hence not suicide, because his death did not result from his action in the right way. One condition which would exclude this sort of case is the requirement that the action be generated in the way that the agent believed it would be generated if it is to be intentional (in either sense). If, following Goldman, we call the agent's act-generational beliefs his action-plan, then this is just Goldman's requirement that the actual causal chain conform to the agent's action-plan.

Though this requirement seems to provide a plausible account of why the above self-caused death is not intentional, and hence why it is not a suicide, it seems to be too strong. It is not plausible to suppose that any deviation, however slight, between the actual course of events and the agent's action-plan is sufficient to render an action nonintentional.

Suppose a person has decided to commit suicide by shooting himself in the head but that when the occasion arises his hand shakes so severely that he shoots himself in the heart. Clearly this person has committed suicide even though the way he intended his death to come about does not exactly coincide with the way his death did come about.[18] Some level of conformity between an agent's action-plan and the actual course of events seems to be required even though an exact fit between the two is not. Thus we are still left with the problem of explaining just what makes a particular causal chain a deviant causal chain.[19] Until this problem in the theory of action is satisfactorily resolved, we will not be in a position to say whether particular self-caused deaths which result from causal chains which do not exactly coincide with the agent's action-plan are suicides or not.

This analysis of suicide is clearly preferable to the alternatives discussed above; it provides a reasonably clear account of what makes a self-caused death a suicide. Since the definition is framed in terms of the concept of intentional action, it is to be expected that our lack of a complete analysis of this concept will give rise to problem cases. But this fact is no reason for objecting to the analysis. In the first place, the respect in which the analysis of intentional action is incomplete does not affect our ability to draw a clear distinction between strongly and weakly intentional action. Second, the definition, by showing how the concept of suicide can be understood in terms of the concept of intentional action, has reduced two problems to one; the problem of determining whether these problem cases are genuine cases of suicide is seen to be nothing other than the problem of determining whether the self-caused death is intentional. Finally, the problem which remains, that of distinguishing deviant from nondeviant causal chains, is a general problem which faces a number of otherwise plausible theories. Thus we may hope that a solution to it in any of the contexts in which it has arisen will prove applicable in other contexts as well.

NOTES

1. Emile Durkheim, *Suicide,* trans. Spaulding and Simpson, (Glencoe, Ill.: The Free Press, 1951).
2. R. B. Brandt, "The Morality and Rationality of Suicide," *A Handbook for the Study of Suicide,* ed. Seymour Perlin (Oxford, 1975), reprinted in Battin and Mayo, eds., *Suicide: The Philosophical Issues* (New York, 1980), pp. 117–32, [see chapter 15 in this volume].
3. Durkheim, p. 44.
4. Brandt (1975), p. 117.
5. The distinction between active and passive suicide is analogous to the distinction between active and passive euthanasia and is equally problematic since it is based on the killing/letting die distinction.
6. Joseph Margolis, *Negativities: The Limits of Life* (Columbus, 1975), pp. 23–36.
7. Tom L. Beauchamp, "Suicide," *Matters of Life and Death,* ed. Tom Regan (New York, 1980), p. 76.
8. Ibid., p. 77.
9. Ibid., p. 72.
10. "Did Socrates Commit Suicide?" *Philosophy* 53 (1978): 106–108 [see this volume, chapter 5].
11. Izuma, Takedo, et al., *Chushingura,* trans. Donald Keene (New York, 1971-2).
12. Case F is tricky. I would contend that although the sadist has coerced Brown into choosing between these options, he has not coerced him into killing himself. However, whether I am right about this is irrelevant to the point at issue.
13. It is true that Beauchamp's definition requires the agent to bring about his death intentionally. But he does not explain what he takes this requirement to involve. So far as I can tell, he seems to be using the term in the weak sense discussed below.
14. See, for example, Alvin I. Goldman, *A Theory of Human Action* (Englewood Cliffs, N.J.· Prentice Hall, 1970), (hereafter referred to as *THA*).
15. Some controversy surrounds the question of whether actions (a)–(e) are

distinct. I shall assume, contra Anscombe and Davidson, that Goldman's arguments for an affirmative answer are sound. Those who disagree may well be able to restate the views expressed in this section so as to avoid this assumption.

16. For a more detailed account of act-generation see *THA*, pp. 20–48.

17. This definition is modeled on Goldman's definition of intentional action (*THA*, p. 57).

18. I am indebted to Michael Tye for this example. A similar case is discussed by Castañeda, "Intensionality and Contingent Identity in Human Action," *Nous* 13 (May 1979): 254–55.

19. For promising attempts to resolve this problem see Christopher Peacocke's "Deviant Causal Chains," *Midwest Studies in Philosophy* 4 (1979): 123–53; and Michael H. Robins, "Deviant Causal Chains and Non-Basic Action," unpublished. A version of this article was read at the Eastern Division meetings of the American Philosophical Association, Boston, Mass., December 27, 1980.

8

The Rhetoric of Suicide

Suzanne Stern-Gillet

In this paper I intend to draw attention to one aspect of the concept of suicide, namely, what I shall call its "responsibility-ascribing" function. In view of the lively controversy generated by R. G. Frey's contention that Socrates committed suicide,[1] I shall use the case of Socrates as a convenient thread to run through my argument. Though I hope, in the process, to shed some light on the way we view the death of Socrates, it is not my main purpose in this paper to solve the problem of describing correctly his manner of death.

True enough, Socrates died, literally, "by his own hand": he knew what he was doing when he lifted the hemlock to his lips and he could (in one sense of "could," at any rate) have escaped into exile. Nevertheless I want to deny that most of us should want to call him a suicide. My ground is that any definition of suicide (such as Durkheim's or Frey's) which allows for Socrates' inclusion in this class is incomplete insofar as it blurs important distinctions between what are, in fact, different *manners of viewing* a person's death. To claim, as Frey does, that Socrates

From *Philosophy and Rhetoric* 20, No. 3 (1987): 160–70. Copyright 1987 by The Pennsylvania State University. Reproduced by permission of The Pennsylvania State University Press.

committed suicide amounts to a disregard of the practical function and, therewith, the rhetorical connotation(s) of the concept of "suicide."

DURKHEIM, FREY, AND HOLLAND

In Durkheim's words: "The term *suicide is applied to all cases* of death resulting directly or indirectly from a positive or negative act of the victim himself, which he knows will produce this result."[2] This definition, by doing away with motives and intentions, led Durkheim to term suicides acts which are not normally so classified. As he wrote: ". . . if the intention of self-destruction alone constituted suicide, the name 'suicide' could not be given to acts which, despite apparent differences, are fundamentally identical with those always called suicide and which could not be otherwise described without discarding the term. The soldier facing certain death to save his regiment does not wish to die, and yet is he not as much the author of his own death as the manufacturer or merchant who kills himself to avoid bankruptcy? This holds true for the martyr dying for his faith, the mother sacrificing herself for her child, etc. Whether death is accepted merely as an unfortunate consequence, but inevitable given the purpose, or is actually itself sought and desired, in either case the person renounces existence, and the various methods of doing so can only be varieties of a single class. . . . Thus, when resolution entails certain sacrifice of life, scientifically this is a suicide. . . ."[3] Though he expresses concern not to go "counter" to ordinary usage,[4] Durkheim is resolved not to be deterred if the resulting class "fails to include all cases ordinarily included under the name or includes others usually otherwise classified."[5] Thus he presents martyrdom as a mere species of the genus "suicide."

R. G. Frey defines suicide as the act of "killing oneself intentionally, or self-murder."[6] He follows this up by asserting that: ". . . Socrates did plainly commit suicide. For he drank the hemlock knowingly, not unknowingly, or in ignorance of what its effect on him would be, and intentionally, not accidentally or mistakenly; and he died as a result of his act of drinking the hemlock."[7] The main difference between Durkheim's and Frey's definitions is that, unlike Durkheim, Frey has the concept of intention play a central role. As to calling Socrates' death a suicide, there is, however, no difference between the two authors, though the case is not explicitly mentioned by Durkheim. Indeed, since he allows the death of one who "accepts death merely as an unfortunate consequence" to be classified as a suicide, Durkheim clearly would have agreed with Frey's contention.

R. F. Holland, who reproaches Durkheim with not having "understood what suicide is,"[8] specifically raises the following objection: "On this account of the matter it looks as if we have to say that a man who exposes himself to mortal danger, for whatever reason and whatever the circumstances, is exposing himself to suicide."[9] Thus extended, the class of suicide, claims Holland, would include not only Captain Oates and Socrates but also, in general, all cases usually understood as "altruistic suicides" (though not in Durkheim's sense of this expression).[10] This seems to constitute a cause of worry for Holland, whose purpose it is to examine the "ethico-religious status of self-slaughter."[11] Indeed, insofar as he is reluctant to allow that suicide can be morally commendable Holland has an axe to grind. This becomes clear when he deals with the hypothetical example of a spy who, on his impending capture, kills himself to avoid betraying his comrades: ". . . the spy . . . is concerned solely with the good of others. *Because of this* one would like to deny that his is the spirit of suicide."[12] Further on, discussing the case of Captain Oates, Holland writes: "The sentiment that he was entitled to quit, or that anyway he was going to quit, never entered into it. Accordingly, I want to deny that he was a suicide."[13] Later in the same paragraph, Holland startlingly asserts that Oates didn't kill himself but that "the blizzard killed him."[14]

DIFFICULTIES IN THE ABOVE DEFINITIONS

While Durkheim is, in my view, correct in claiming that a suicide rightly so-called need not have taken an active part in his or her own death, the definition he proposes leads to a questionable broadening of the concept of suicide. It would include not only clear cases of self-sacrifice and martyrdom but also more borderline cases such as those of Socrates, Jesus, and, probably, Bobby Sands.[15] Furthermore, as I hope to show presently, it seems doubtful whether the existence of the class of suicide can be determined "scientifically."

Though Frey mentions Socrates' wish to die, he centers his argument on the surely trifling fact that Socrates "did not drink the hemlock against his will"[16] and, therefore, took an *active* part in his own death. Frey has been criticized for this justificatory move. As Michael Smith convincingly argued, drinking the hemlock intentionally does not entail killing oneself intentionally.[17] Besides, if a person's *active participation* in bringing about his own death be needed for calling him a suicide then a mention of Socrates' second address to the court[18] would surely have been more to the point.

As to Holland's objection to the extension of the class of suicide, I agree with the substance of it though not with its grounds. Almost without exception Holland considers suicide to be morally wrong; however, this alleged moral wrongness is hardly the reason why we are reluctant to accept the view that Socrates, the patron saint of philosophers, committed suicide. Or should we not be so reluctant? Anyway, why should the possibility of "altruistic suicides" be almost ruled out? Surely Holland would not deny that Oates deserves praise for walking into the blizzard. If Oates didn't deliberately go to his death and if it was the blizzard that "killed him," what do we praise him for? Should we rather praise the blizzard?

THE DEATH OF JESUS

Is it only "piety" that prevents us from viewing Jesus' death as a suicide? Indeed, if we read the Gospels with the question, "Did Jesus intend his own death?" a positive answer appears almost inevitable. Early on in his public life Jesus told the assembled disciples that ". . . the son of man must suffer many things, and be rejected by the elders and the chief priests and the scribes, and be killed, and after three days rise again."[19] Later on, in the narrative of the Passion, Matthew reports the episode of Jesus being taken captive by the soldiers of the chief priests and rebuking one of them who had drawn his sword: "Put your sword back into its place; for all who take the sword will perish by the sword. Do you think that I cannot appeal to my Father, and he will at once send me more than twelve legions of angels? But how then should the scriptures be fulfilled, that it must be so?"[20]

Prophecies such as Isaiah's,[21] to which the passage in Matthew is an allusion, were well known to the Jews. We can take the view either that Jesus was indeed the son of God or that he was but a historical figure well-known at the time for various claims he made. In the first case His deliberate refraining from seeking help from the "legions of angels" appears like an acceptance of death, albeit for the sake of His redeeming mission. This would make Him a suicide, sub-class martyrdom, in Durkheim's classification. Though for reasons that have nothing to do with "piety," I shall argue that such a description of Jesus' death is rather misleading.

On the other hand, if we view Jesus' death from outside the Christian perspective, what we have is a man who seeks to convince others that he is more than he might appear, in fact that he is the Messiah of whom the prophets spoke. How better can he prove this than by making the prophecies come true? His death becomes the supreme argument: he proves himself to be what he claims to be *only* if he dies. After all the claims he had made in the course of his public life, Jesus had no option but to make sure that he was condemned to death. Should we call this partly self-engineered martyrdom a suicide?

There are interesting parallels between the death of Jesus and that of Socrates. In the course of their trial both defiantly stood by what they had formerly taught, while being fully aware that a condemnation to death would ensue. In neither case does it seem far-fetched to say that they provoked the Court into condemning them to death. It is true that, unlike Socrates, Jesus didn't die by his own hand. However, as was pointed out earlier against Frey, this difference isn't really significant. It would seem, therefore, that the claims that Socrates as well as Jesus committed suicide are either to stand or to fall together.

The fact that many would balk at the idea that Jesus committed suicide no doubt shows that this is still in some sense a Christian society and that the concept of suicide has, therefore, retained a derogatory connotation. However, there is another, more fundamental and, I should contend, perfectly legitimate reason for our reluctance to place either figure in the class of "suicides." Such a reason stems from a proper appreciation of the rhetoric of the term "suicide."

THE DEATH OF BOBBY SANDS

The rhetoric of suicide can perhaps best be illustrated by the death, in May 1981, of Bobby Sands, the I. R. A. [Irish Republican Army] Provisional who went on a hunger strike in protest against the government's refusal to grant political prisoners' status to himself and his fellow I. R. A. Provisionals in prison. It will be recalled that, in 1972, after an earlier hunger strike, the government had agreed that convicted prisoners claiming a political motive for their 'crimes' should be granted "special category" status. That ruling had been rescinded in 1976.

In the course of his long fast Sands had rejected several appeals to call off his hunger strike on the grounds that he had no reason "to suit

the people who oppress, torture, and imprison me, and who wish to dehu-
manize me. While I remain alive, I remain what I am, a political prisoner
of war."[22] In the same vein Sands's mother was quoted as saying that
her son was "offering his life" for a set of conditions in prison.[23]

In the course of the debate in the House of Commons, subsequent
to the announcement of Sands's death, the Prime Minister said: "He chose
to take his own life, a choice his organization did not allow to any of
its victims."[24] The British establishment mostly took the view that Sands
was a suicide. This view and its implications are most clearly and explicitly spelled out in the *Times* editorial of 6th May, 1981: "By refusing to
submit to Mr. Sands' blackmail, the British Government bears no responsibility whatever for his death. He committed suicide, in full knowledge
of what he was doing and determined to reject all initiatives to save his
life. He was not hounded into death. . . . Every discomfort he endured
leading up to and including his death was self-inflicted. . . . There is only
one killer of Bobby Sands and that is Sands himself." It is interesting
to contrast the tone of this editorial with a pronouncement made by Mr.
Carey, then Governor of the State of New York: "I deeply regret that
the British Government has let Bobby Sands bring his hunger strike to
its bitter conclusion."[25] This remark was taken as an indication that Her
Majesty's government had alienated sections of public opinion abroad.

One major difference between the establishment's various pronounce-
ments, on the one hand, and those of Sands's supporters or, e.g., Governor Carey, on the other hand, is immediately apparent: in the first case
Sands is presented as having the initiative and thus deciding his fate while
in the second case it is the government which is taken to have the initiative
while Sands is at its mercy. In such a case, whoever had the initiative
both bears the responsibility and incurs praise or blame for what happens.
It is thus quite clear why the establishment insisted on putting the label
"suicide" on Sands; to do so amounts to denying a direct causal link between their actions and the event and thus denying responsibility. To say
that Sands committed suicide is to say that he brought about his own
death and, therefore, bears responsibility for it. Equally clearly, Sands's
supporters view his death as directly caused by the government's actions
or lack of action and so they staunchly deny that he was a suicide. They
view him as a martyr.

According to the common conception of martyrdom a death has a
claim to come under the heading of martyrdom when it is deliberately
or intentionally undergone for the sake of one's principles or cause. That

this concept and that of suicide often function as instruments of persuasion comes out clearly in the case of Sands; whether we call him a martyr or a suicide largely depends on how we view, and the role we attribute to, the principles or cause in question. It appears clearly, therefore, that the word 'suicide' has rhetorical associations since, at any rate in cases such as Sands's, to say that a person committed or didn't commit suicide amounts to taking a political stand.

SOCRATES AGAIN

The case of Socrates, obviously, no longer excites the same amount of partisan passions as it did in the fourth century B.C. or as the case of Sands did a few years ago. However, the cases are sufficiently similar for the case of Sands to throw light on the case of Socrates. I want to claim that when Frey calls Socrates a suicide he is, in effect, playing Margaret Thatcher to Bobby Sands's Socrates. He is alleviating the responsibility (and thus the blame) incurred by the Athenian court over the death of Socrates while, correspondingly, stressing Socrates' own responsibility. Polemically, he is on the side of the Athenians since he is, more or less, telling them: "Don't be shamed into believing that you have killed Socrates; in fact, he committed suicide."

In Plato's *Apology* Socrates is rejecting in advance such whitewashing of the authorities when, alluding to his advanced age, he warns the Court that: "It is for the sake of a short time, gentlemen of the jury, that you will acquire the reputation and *the guilt, in the eyes of those who want to denigrate the city,* of having killed Socrates. . . . "[26] Those words, not those of a man bent on self-destruction, are Socrates' way of pointing out to the Court the risks involved in their condemning him to death: he will be viewed as a martyr and the Athenians will be taken to bear responsibility for his death.

THE RHETORIC OF SUICIDE

We are now in a position to spell out one of the differences between martyrdom and suicide. *To call X a suicide amounts, amongst other things, to ascribing to X the moral responsibility (and sometimes, but not always, the blame) for X's death. To call X a martyr amounts, amongst other things, to ascribing the moral responsibility (and, usually, the blame) for X's death to someone else (usually a government, an institution, or an organization).* Of course, as long as, in the manner of Durkheim, one uses purely behavioral criteria there is no way of distinguishing between martyrs and suicides. Recent work on suicide[27] has tended to concentrate on the concept of intention. However, unless they are accompanied by some kind of double effect type of argument, such analyses will be no help in solving the problem raised by Socrates' or any martyr's death. Had it been noticed that the concept of suicide denotes not only a manner of dying but also a way of viewing the broader circumstances of a death, the problem would not have arisen in the first place. The case of Socrates, as the amount of interest generated by Mr. Frey's article testifies, shows quite plainly that the concept of suicide has a very powerful rhetoric of its own.

That the concept of "suicide" has such a "responsibility-ascribing" function appears also from the fact that in most penal systems great care is taken that a prisoner condemned to death shouldn't kill himself in his cell. In fact, should he fall ill, he will first be nursed back to health before being executed. For several reasons it is considered important that the prisoner should be executed and not come under the heading of "suicide" or "natural death." What light this observation throws on the penal systems in question is not a problem that need concern us here.

The foregoing remarks on responsibility should not be taken as ruling out of court the possibility of "induced suicides." In the case of an "induced suicide" the responsibility (and, most likely, the blame) for X's death falls mainly on whoever induced X to bring about his or her own death. The existence of induced suicides, however, does not invalidate my general claim; in such cases it is usually made clear that the "suicide" was "driven to it" or, indeed, that he or she was a suicide between quotation marks. Besides, such was obviously not in the case of Socrates or, for that matter, of Jesus.

I do not want to suggest either that it is conceptually impossible that one and the same death could be both a suicide and a condemnation to death though it would be a case of over-determination. Might Seneca be an example in point? It would seem so, at any rate, from the account of J. R. G. Wright: "In 65 he was accused of participation in a conspiracy to depose Nero (some said he was to succeed to the throne) and, on imperial *command, embraced* the suicide which his philosophy *permitted* him as a final release from the ills of this world."[28] In view of the fact that he was ordered to commit suicide but was left the choice of means, and anyway belonged to a philosophical persuasion not inimical to suicide, Seneca falls somewhat uneasily between the case of the prisoner condemned to death and the case of the suicide. Though he wasn't a prisoner and hadn't, strictly speaking, been condemned to death, the political circumstances in Rome at that time made Nero's order amount to condemnation to death. Though Seneca's stoicism meant that he didn't have any objection in principle to dying by his own hand, he was in fact given the choice between killing himself and being killed by soldiers of the Pretorian Guard.

Clearly, in the absence of any qualifications, the epithet "suicide" does not fit the death of Seneca. Intuitively, we recognize this when we say, e.g., that Seneca was *"forced* to commit suicide"; we resort to paradox to lessen the inadequacy of the description. In fact, we do want to make the point that responsibility for Seneca's death is to be laid wholly at Nero's door; though it was not contrary to Seneca's principles to die as he did, he died when he did because Nero had decreed that he should. Seneca didn't open his veins either from philosophical conviction or because he was tired of life: he had, in effect, been condemned to death but was allowed to choose how to die.

In conclusion I should want to claim that: (1) the notion of suicide has a practical function or meaning, namely, that of ascribing moral responsibility; and (2) this practical function is not an adventitious adjunct to the so-called descriptive meaning of the concept of suicide but is an integral part of it. In fact, the two aspects, i.e., the descriptive and the practical, are, in this case, inextricably intermingled. What I have called throughout this paper the "rhetoric of suicide" stems from this practical function: if it is, indeed, the case that to call X a suicide is to locate in X him/herself the main responsibility for his or her death, then the question as to whether any particular X was or was not a suicide can become a matter of bitter debate and protracted argument, with no "objective" decision at the end of it. Durkheim hoped that his definition of suicide, by doing away with mental concepts, would allow individual cases to be settled "scientifically" and unambiguously. Besides the difficulties raised by Holland, it should be stressed that the concept of suicide, *de facto,* reflects the views and attitudes of the society or group who apply it to individual instances. As such both "suicide" and "martyrdom" are incapable of being "scientifically" determined.

This *practical* or responsibility-ascribing function of the concept is not to be confused with what Stevenson called the "emotional meaning." Clearly the word "suicide" has, from certain religious points of view and in many people's minds, a derogatory emotive connotation. Since they take suicide to be morally wrong they feel a corresponding reluctance to make conceptual room for "altruistic suicide." The curious reluctance shown by several philosophers to describe Captain Oates's death as a suicide shows this. In fact, Frey's claim might arguably be viewed, Stevenson fashion, as an attempt at a persuasive definition. By extending the denotation of the concept of "suicide" so that it now includes Socrates, Frey is making an attempt at altering its emotive meaning. Frey's concluding remark lends weight to this interpretation: ". . . the fact that Socrates died a noble and dignified death does not show that he did not commit suicide, but rather that suicide need not be ignoble and undignified."[29] Quite so. But it doesn't show, either, of course, that Socrates did commit suicide. Where Mr. Frey's argument seems to me to misfire is due to his neglect of the responsibility-locating aspect of the concept of suicide.

If my contention concerning the practical function of the concept of suicide is accepted, it will clear suicide of its present negative emotive coloring, while at the same time retaining the important insight that the concept of "suicide" is not purely descriptive. Indeed, since the concept has the practical function of ascribing moral responsibility, such responsibility will be ascribed for moral deeds as well as for immoral ones. We need feel no compunction in describing Captain Oates as a suicide. Suicide can, indeed, be noble and dignified. In order to make this point, however, there is no need to include Socrates in the class of suicides.

NOTES

1. R. G. Frey, "Did Socrates Commit Suicide?" *Philosophy* 53 (1978): 106–108 [see this volume, chapter 5].

2. E. Durkheim, *Suicide,* trans. Spaulding and Simpson (Glencoe, Ill.: The Free Press, 1951), p. 44; 1st ed. 1897.

3. Ibid., pp. 43–44.

4. Ibid., p. 42.

5. Ibid.

6. Frey, p. 106 [see this volume, chapter 5, p. 57].

7. Ibid.

8. R. F. Holland, "Suicide," repr. in *Against Empiricism* (Totowa, N.J.: Barnes and Noble Books, 1980), pp. 143–57.

9. Ibid., p. 144.

10. Holland, p. 221. Durkheim calls "altruistic suicides" or, more specifically, "obligatory altruistic suicides," those that are committed, under compelling reasons imposed by their societies, on (1) men on the threshold of old age or stricken with disease, (2) women on their husband's death, and (3) followers or servants on the death of their chief or master. These cases Durkheim considers to exhibit the essential characteristics of altruistic suicide, while "other varieties are only derivative forms" (Holland, p. 240).

11. Ibid., p. 146.

12. Ibid., p. 149.

13. Ibid.

14. Ibid., p. 151.

15. I say "probably" because it could be argued that Sands couldn't "know" that his hunger strike would result in his own death since he must have hoped, at the very least initially, that the government would accede to his request.

16. Frey, p. 106 [see this volume, chapter 5, p. 57].

17. Michael Smith, "Did Socrates Kill Himself Intentionally?" *Philosophy* 55 (1980): 253–54; Holland, p. 146, had earlier made a similar point when he had remarked that "Taking hemlock, . . . in the context of an Athenian judicial execution, . . . is no more an act of suicide than the condemned man's walk to the scaffold."

18. Plato, *Apology,* 36d–38b.

19. Mark 8:31.

20. Matthew 26:52–53.

21. Chs. 42 and 49.

22. Quoted in *Time* magazine, 4th May, 1981.

23. Quoted in *The Times,* 4th May, 1981.

24. Quoted in *The Times,* 6th May, 1981.

25. Quoted in *New York Times* of 5th May, 1981.

26. Plato, *Apology,* 38c (my italics).

27. Cf., for instance, R. A. Duff, "Socratic Suicide?" *Proceedings of the Aristotelian Society,* 1982–83.

28. J. R. G. Wright, "Seneca," in P. Edwards, ed., *The Encyclopaedia of Philosophy* (New York: The Macmillan Company and The Free Press, 1967). My italics.

29. Frey, p. 108 [see this volume, chapter 5, p. 59].

9

Suicide and Self-Inflicted Death

R. G. Frey

The most common view of suicide today is that it is intentional self-kill-ing.[1] Because of the self-killing component, suicide is often described as self-inflicted death or as dying by one's own hand, and the victim is in turn often described as having done himself to death or as having taken his own life. But must one's death be self-inflicted in order to be suicide? The answer, I want to suggest, is arguably no.

I

In many cases of suicide, death is obviously self-inflicted; I refer, of course, to cases where the individual shoots himself or cuts his wrists or commits hara-kiri. It is equally obvious, however, that there are dozens of cases of what we take to be suicide where death is not self-inflicted in this nar-row sense. If Jones wants to die and throws himself under a train, I take it that all of us want to regard him as a suicide, even though it is the train which actually kills him. How, then, do we do this? The answer,

From *Philosophy* 56 (1981): 193–202. Copyright © Royal Institute of Philosophy. Re-printed with the permission of Cambridge University Press.

of course, is that we distinguish this narrow sense of "self-inflicted" from a broad sense, according to which one's death is self-inflicted if one wants to die, knowingly and willingly places oneself in perilous circumstances, and dies as a result.[2] Thus, Jones, who wants to die, knowingly and willingly places himself in circumstances where his death, if not actually inevitable, at least is exceedingly likely, and he dies as a result; he commits suicide, therefore, even though his death is not self-inflicted in the narrow sense.

I shall not bother with the secondary issue of how perilous the circumstances must be before one is deemed a suicide. There is almost certainly, however, a lower limit to perilousness. If instead of throwing himself under a train Jones takes a scheduled flight from London to New York, and if the plane goes down, I should still not want to say that Jones committed suicide. For apart from anything else, though he knowingly and willingly takes this flight, flying the Atlantic on a scheduled flight is not sufficiently perilous—the odds on any single such plane going down are simply too low—to make Jones a suicide.

Merely placing oneself in perilous circumstances and dying as a result, however, does not make one a suicide; one must also want to die. Soldiers who volunteer for hazardous war-time missions knowingly and willingly place themselves in perilous circumstances; but their deaths do not amount to suicide, any more than do those of traffic wardens in Rome, who go into the midst of and vainly try to direct rush-hour traffic. (There is a use of 'suicide' in which engaging or persisting in a course of action in perilous circumstances is likened to suicide, even though there is no question of the agent actually wanting to die. A soldier in the trenches who says "To go over the top now is suicide" or who, upon returning from the front, says "It's suicide up there," in fact means that the likelihood of death is very considerably increased by going over the top or to the front, not that all soldiers who so act when ordered commit suicide, if they are killed.)

II

The broad sense of "self-inflicted" death helps in some cases with the vexing problem of whether sacrificial deaths are suicides.[3] R. F. Holland has maintained that Captain Oates, who walked away from Scott's camp in the Antarctic rather than continue through illness to be a burden on the expedition, did not commit suicide, since he did not shoot or eviscerate himself but simply walked off into the freezing cold, which eventually killed him.[4] On the broad sense of "self-inflicted" death, however, Oates certainly did commit suicide, however noble his motive for doing what he did; indeed, on this sense, his motive is irrelevant to whether he committed suicide. For he knowingly and willingly placed himself in circumstances where he would die, and he died as a result; and though it is the freezing cold which actually killed him, he put himself in precisely those circumstances where it would kill him. The only question, then, is whether Oates wanted to die, and we can reasonably infer from his intentionally (not accidentally or mistakenly) walking off, together with his knowledge of what the effect of this on him would be, that he did indeed want to die, if not as an end, at least as a means to the end of allowing Scott to carry on unencumbered. One might argue, I suppose, that though Captain Oates foresaw as a consequence of walking off that he would die, what he wanted was not to die but to allow Scott to carry on unencumbered; but it is equally reasonable to argue that, having taken stock of his situation and Scott's, Oates wanted to die *in order to* allow Scott to carry on.[5]

(Doubtless Oates considered his options carefully and came to the decision to walk off; but deliberation and explicit decision are not necessary in order that one knowingly and willingly do something. I knowingly and willingly come into work each morning, but I certainly do not normally deliberate doing so and decide accordingly, just as I can knowingly and willingly go to the cinema without deliberating the merits of possible alternatives and explicitly deciding on this alternative as opposed to some other.)

Cases of sacrificial death, however, come in all shapes and sizes, and though the broad sense of "self-inflicted" death helps with some, it cannot be seen as the solution to all such cases. A soldier who throws himself on a live grenade, in order to save his comrades, commits suicide, if we can agree that (i) he knowingly and willingly acts as he does, and (ii) he wants to die, if not as an end, at least as a means. The fly in the ointment, of course, is our agreeing upon (i) and (ii). In some cases, (i) and (ii) may be reasonably clear. A father who gives his sole remaining kidney in order to save the life of his young son and who dies as a result, pretty clearly satisfies (i) and (ii). Our initial hesitation, such as it is, over (ii) stems from the fact that, were his son not ill, the father would not contemplate giving up his life; but his son is ill, and if the son can only live with the kidney and the father cannot live without the kidney, then in giving up his kidney to save his son the father consents to his own death as the means to that end. This does not mean that he welcomes death, but it does mean that he not merely foresees his death but also takes steps to bring it about and approves the result it achieves. In the case of the soldier, on the other hand, there are complicating factors, not the least serious of which is time. In respect of (i), knowingly and willingly acting as he does, the whole incident may occur so quickly that the soldier behaves spontaneously and unthinkingly; and though we may be reluctant to say that he acts accidentally or mistakenly, we may be equally reluctant to maintain that, in acting spontaneously and unthinkingly, he acts knowingly and willingly. In respect to (ii), wanting to die, if the whole incident is over and done with in a few seconds, we may be reluctant to say of the soldier that he wanted anything, at least in any occurrent sense of that term. Certainly we should be reluctant to speak of his "deciding" to act as he does and so as a result coming to want to die.

So far as the time-factor is concerned, then, I suspect that the more spontaneous the act can be made to appear, as in the case of the soldier, the less likely we shall be to consider the victim a suicide, whereas the less spontaneous the act appears, as in the case of the father, the more likely we shall be to construe sacrificial deaths as suicides. In the light of this, it is no accident that those cases of sacrificial death most seized upon in the literature and held not to be suicide are precisely those in which the agent at once falls upon a grenade or dashes into a blazing house or dives into a raging sea. Just because of the time-factor, these cases appear to put maximum stress on the broad sense of "self-inflicted" death, as an aid to sorting out sacrificial deaths.

Yet, even these spontaneous cases are open to a difficulty of sorts, in their use against the broad view of "self-inflicted" death. The problem is not that spontaneous (and unthinking) acts cannot be meritorious; on the contrary, I can well imagine someone arguing that the good man is one who, in certain circumstances, does not think and calculate but acts out of ingrained good habits and/or principles. So to speak, the man of good character just does the right thing in these cases, spontaneously and uncalculatedly.[6] No, the problem with such cases is that, the more spontaneous they are made to appear, in order to avoid their succumbing to the broad sense of "self-inflicted" death, the more like reflex actions they become; and the more like reflex actions they become, the less likely we shall be to say of the agents that they acted at all. A reflex knee-jerk is not an act in the operative sense, and if falling upon the grenade or dashing into the blazing building or diving into the raging sea is made out to be so spontaneous as to approximate to a knee-jerk, then it is arguable that the agent has not acted at all, in the operative sense. In short, then, in order to avoid being instances of suicide on the broad sense of "self-inflicted" death, these cases of sacrificial death must appear to include a considerable degree of spontaneity in the act of the agent; but in order to avoid their appearing as instances of reflex action and so of not amounting to acts in the operative sense, the degree of spontaneity in the act of the agent must be restricted. I am not suggesting that these two demands are altogether and always incompatible, only that they impose limits on the types of cases of sacrificial death that can be used to evade the broad sense of "self-inflicted" death.

III

If suicide, then, is killing oneself intentionally, one must not interpret this expression so narrowly as to preclude self-inflicted deaths in the broad sense from being suicides. This is why the tendency to use the expressions "dying by one's own hand" and "self-inflicted death" interchangeably of suicide is so very unfortunate; for if all those cases of dying by one's own hand are cases of self-inflicted death (in the narrow sense), not all cases of self-inflicted death (i.e., those in the broad sense) are cases of dying by one's own hand. In the broad sense of self-inflicted death, something in the circumstances kills one, such as a train; and being run over by a train is not dying by one's own hand, a phrase which is typically used to single out an individual's own act of swallowing poison or cutting his wrists.

Now the cases we have in mind to cover by means of the broad sense of self-inflicted death are just those, like the cases of Jones and Captain Oates, where what it is in the circumstances which actually produces death is something like a train or a car or the weather or a fire. But what if the circumstances into which one places oneself, with death as a practically certain outcome, involve fundamentally an explicit and overt act on the part of another human being? If the victim dies as a result of this other person's act, can he be a suicide? The broad sense of "self-inflicted" death was not intended to and does not obviously cover such cases, and it seems reasonable to maintain that, if one dies as the result of another party's act, one's death is not self-inflicted in any sense. Therefore, if we are prepared to allow that the individual in question nevertheless commits suicide, it follows that suicide does not require self-inflicted death.

But *are* we prepared to allow that such an individual commits suicide? I think there are cases where we *will* allow this, unless we go on to regard them as cases of both suicide *and* murder or manslaughter by another party; for there are features to these cases which make it highly doubtful that we shall regard them as cases of murder or manslaughter pure and simple.

The limits within which such cases must fall can be garnered from a more straightforward case in which the victim is killed by another person. In a detective story I read not long ago, Bill and Bob are performing in a play one scene of which calls for Bill to take a pistol from a drawer and shoot Bob. The pistol has always been loaded with blanks, of course, but on the evening in question, when Bill once again takes up the gun and shoots Bob, Bob really is killed. The novelist heightens the tension surrounding the ensuing investigation, first, by presenting evidence that Bob was depressed and under considerable strain, and second, by presenting evidence that he was hated by a number of his fellow players, including Bill.

Three features of this case are important here. First, there is no doubt whatever that Bob has been shot and killed by Bill. It does not follow, however, that Bob did not commit suicide. For he knew that the pistol would be fired by Bill directly at him; and if Bob was the one who loaded the pistol with live bullets, then the police will conclude that Bob committed suicide, even though Bill killed him. If, however, Bill or a third party loaded the pistol, then the police will conclude that Bob was murdered. Thus, the determination of whether Bob committed suicide is made to depend, not upon who actually shot and killed Bob, but upon who loaded the pistol. Second, if Bob loaded the pistol, he has contrived his death in such a way that he ends up dead at the hands of another person. For merely loading the pistol with live bullets does not issue in the death of Bob; Bill must also pull the trigger of the pistol. Third, though Bob's death is obviously not self-inflicted in the narrow sense, it is arguable that, if he loaded the pistol, this fact suffices to render his death self-inflicted in the broad sense. At the very least, he takes a hand in his own death, not in some indirect or remote sense, but in the wholly direct and immediate sense of knowingly and willingly loading the gun which, given the scene in the play, in all likelihood will kill him.

What this case teaches us is that, if we are to find a case of other-inflicted death which is nevertheless arguably a case of suicide, what we must come up with is a case not only where the victim, who contrives his death, is killed by someone else, but also where he does not perform an act comparable to that of loading the pistol, such as switching the capsules or disguising the poison which kills him. For acts of this sort appear compatible with the broad sense of self-inflicted death. (I shall not consider cases of begging and pleading with someone to kill one, since acts of this kind, by a person who is seriously and painfully ill, raise questions beyond the scope of this paper.) Are there any cases, therefore, which satisfy these requirements? I believe that there are.

IV

In a film I saw as a young boy, Ted, an aging cowboy who is down on his luck, decides to end it all. He does not suffer from any disease and is not otherwise approaching a "vegetable" condition; he is simply miserable and unhappy. In one scene, he puts a loaded pistol to his head but cannot bring himself to pull the trigger. Therefore, he devises a plan: he will challenge his worst enemy, a well-known outlaw, to meet him at high noon, in the knowledge that the outlaw cannot refuse without serious loss of face (quite apart from the fact that refusal exposes *him* to possible death from *his* enemies) and that the outlaw is both fast and accurate with a gun. Ted further plans, if he does manage to draw his gun, not to fire it. The plan is put into effect, the two meet, and Ted is killed. Does Ted commit suicide? Or does the outlaw murder him?

The case for suicide is readily apparent: Ted wants to die and carefully plans his death; he puts this plan into operation and thereby knowingly and willingly places himself in a situation where death is a practical certainty; and he dies as a result. The outcome, in other words, is precisely what he hopes, wants, and plans it to be. The case for murder is equally apparent: the outlaw does not have to accept Ted's challenge or meet him in the street or draw his gun or shoot or kill Ted; and it would be false to think that Ted's death is an accident.

To someone who wanted to regard the case as *obviously* one of murder, what is one to make of Ted's carefully conceived plan and the steps he takes to implement it? One might say, I suppose, that Ted's plan is to bring about or force his own murder; but there are two difficulties with this. First, it suggests that it is a part of Ted's plan that the outlaw come to will Ted's death; but this is not the case. All that matters to Ted is that he end up dead at the hands of the outlaw; and if this can be achieved without the outlaw willing his death then, from Ted's point of view, so be it. Second, therefore, if what Ted is doing is planning his own death, as it certainly is, then the essence of this plan consists in manipulating another human being into circumstances where he will kill Ted. Ted does this because he wants to die. Why, then, if death ensues, is Ted not a suicide? He wants to die, plans his death, carefully puts his plan into operation, and dies. If the only reason why he is not a suicide is that he does not actually kill himself, then neither do Jones or Captain Oates actually kill themselves; and if one can be a suicide and be killed by a train or the weather, why can one not be a suicide and be killed by another person?

Our central worry on this score, I think, is that the other person may have come to will the victim's death. But what if the other person *does not* will the victim's death? Is there then any reason for denying that it is a case of suicide? For example, though it is possible simply to lay down that anyone in the outlaw's position who becomes embroiled in Ted's plan comes to will Ted's death, there is something artificial about such a stipulation. In *Imputed Criminal Intent, D. P. P. v. Smith* (London: Her Majesty's Stationery Office, 1967), the Law Commission came out against an objective, hypothetical test of intention, which turns upon what a reasonable man would or would not have foreseen as a consequence of his act, and in favor of a subjective test, which concerns itself with the actual state of mind of the agent, not the hypothetical state of mind of some hypothetical individual. If we adopt some sort of distinction like this for willing another's death, if we then concern ourselves with the other person's actual state of mind, and if that person does not come to will the victim's death, then the major impediment of allowing Ted's case to be suicide is removed. I am not, of course, asserting that the outlaw did not will Ted's death, only that, if he did not, then there appears no reason not to concede this case of other-inflicted death to be suicide.

Consider this case: Tom, who is simply miserable and unhappy, seriously wants to end it all. He has already tried twice to kill himself with a revolver but failed. To ensure success, therefore, he devises a plan: he begins to goad and taunt, to ridicule and humiliate his wife, whom he knows to be of an exceedingly nervous, fragile temperament; and over many weeks his goading, etc., supplemented by beatings, reach fever pitch. His wife is unable to escape the barrage, and, as it grows ever more intense, she reaches the end of her endurance. In a passion, she kills Tom, though she certainly knows what she is doing and realizes full well that a bullet through the heart will kill someone.

In this case, Tom has exploited his wife's temperament in order to bring about his own demise. It is just this exploitation, just this passion which issues in her killing him, and just this outcome which Tom has carefully planned and in the event successfully achieved.

True, the whole episode takes weeks, and it may be suggested, therefore, that Tom's wife has the opportunity to contemplate and plan Tom's death. But what if she does not seize this opportunity? Is there then any reason for denying the case is one of suicide? One can here, too, simply stipulate that anyone in Tom's wife's situation must at least contemplate, if not deliberate, her husband's death; but a stipulation of this sort rings hollow, just because there is no reason, either in logic or in fact, why it must be the case that she contemplates or deliberates or plans Tom's death. Surely, therefore, we must examine her case very closely in order to determine whether she did any of these things. And if she did not, why should we not allow the case to be one of suicide?

Finally, what about planning one's death so that one is killed by what amounts to a reflex action? Consider this case: Tex seriously wants to end it all. He cannot face shooting himself or cutting his wrists, however, so he devises a plan by which someone else kills him. He purchases a gun and blanks and then threatens to kill his small son. When the police arrive, he releases his son and then dashes into a neighboring warehouse, firing his gun as he runs. Once inside the warehouse, he hides behind a large crate, waiting for one of the policemen to come in after him and to get in front of him. When this happens, Tex jumps out from behind the crate, yells an obscenity, waits for the policeman to turn, and then fires one of his blanks. The policeman whirls round, comes face to face with Tex's gun, and instinctively squeezes off his own, only a split second after Tex has fired. Tex is killed.

One might claim that the policeman's initial drawing of his gun indicates a readiness to use it; but to any witness of the above events, his use of the gun was instinctual, a reflex action, in the actual killing of Tex. It is very important to realize, moreover, that the success of Tex's plan *depends upon* a certain readiness by the policeman to use his gun; for he knows that, if policemen were prepared to allow guns repeatedly to be fired at them from point-blank range without defending themselves, his plan would stand no chance whatever of success. Just as Ted exploits the outlaw's reluctance to lose face and to appear in his enemies' eyes as no longer prepared to fight, and just as Tom exploits his wife's fragile temperament, so Tex exploits the policeman's readiness to defend himself.

V

Can one, therefore, commit suicide by planning one's death in such a way that another person kills one? The cases of Ted, Tom, and Tex suggest to me that one can. What, I think, makes them cases of suicide, in spite of the fact that the relevant deaths are not self-inflicted in any sense, is a set of features they all share. Each victim wants to die, and each takes steps to bring this about; each draws up a plan with his death as the outcome; each puts his plan into operation and so knowingly and willingly places himself in circumstances where another person is exceedingly likely to kill him; each exploits and actively manipulates both the circumstances and the other person to this end; each is killed. To leave out these common features in considering these cases is impossible, since they are integral features of them; but to include such features in our consideration of them makes it difficult to conclude that they are cases of murder/manslaughter pure and simple. What this indicates, I think, is that, if the perilous circumstances into which the victim knowingly and willingly places himself involve another person's act, as the result of which the victim dies, then the mere fact that he is killed by someone else *does not preclude* the possibility of his being a suicide, provided it can be shown that he wanted and planned his death and exploited and manipulated the circumstances and the other person to achieve this end as a part of his plan.

More simply, the above cases are all cases of engineering one's death and in this sense describe different ways of doing away with oneself. True, they are not particularly nice ways of doing away with oneself, since they not merely involve but actively exploit and make use of another person in order to accomplish the deed. As such, they are only likely to appeal to those people, for example, who are squeamish and cannot face the thought of blowing off the tops of their heads or cutting out their entrails. These individuals, therefore, are led to plan and contrive their deaths differently, so that they are killed by someone else; and the plans devised in each case have a high probability of producing the desired result.

Of course, there is another and, perhaps, to some, more tempting way of regarding the cases of Ted, Tom, and Tex. I have raised the question of whether they are cases of suicide or murder/manslaughter by another party; but they may be thought by some *to be both,* that is, to be cases of suicide if looked at from the victim's position and cases of murder/manslaughter if looked at from the other party's position. Regarding them as both, moreover, may seem to fit some people's indecision about them: what makes such people hesitate to conclude that they are cases of murder/manslaughter is the set of common features cited above; but what makes them hesitate to conclude that they are cases of suicide is the fear that the other party may have come to will the victim's death. By regarding these cases as both suicide and murder/manslaughter, they try to take into account and so not lose sight of these disparate elements which are the bases of their indecision.

This way of regarding these cases, obviously, runs up against the assumption that one and the same death cannot be both suicide and murder/manslaughter (by another party). This assumption itself, however, depends upon a presumed contrast between suicide as self-inflicted death and murder/manslaughter as other-inflicted death. But if these examples of mine succeed, they either undermine this assumption or at least make plain that it is an assumption, with limitations and exceptions, since there arguably are cases of suicide where the victim's death is not self-inflicted in any sense but other-inflicted. In a word, the presumed contrast breaks down,[7] with the result that the claim of these cases to be both suicide and murder/manslaughter, if it is to be defeated, cannot be defeated simply by relying upon some contrast between self-inflicted and other-inflicted death as the core difference between suicide and murder/manslaughter.

NOTES

1. See my "Did Socrates Commit Suicide?" *Philosophy* 53 (1978): 106–108, reprinted in *Suicide: Contemporary Philosophical Issues,* M. Pabst Battin and David Mayo (eds.). (New York: St. Martin's Press, 1980) [see chapter 5 in this volume].

2. For a very helpful discussion of this broad sense, to which I am indebted, see T. L. Beauchamp, "What Is Suicide?" in *Ethical Issues in Death* and *Dying,* T. L. Beauchamp and S. Perlin (eds.). (Englewood Cliffs, N.J.: Prentice-Hall, 1978), pp. 97–102.

3. See Beauchamp, pp. 99–101, for his discussion of such cases and the case of Captain Oates.

4. "Suicide," in *Moral Problems*, J. Rachels (ed.). (New York: Harper & Row, 1971), pp. 352–54.

5. I am grateful to Margaret Battin for assistance on this point, though in another context.

6. For a discussion of one such view of the good man, see my "What a Good Man Can Bring Himself to Do," *Journal of Value Inquiry* 12 (1978): 134–41.

7. My point here is a theoretical one. I do not deny that there may be good reasons in practice for using some distinction between self-inflicted and other-inflicted death as a rough and ready difference between suicide and murder.

10

Suicide and Self-Starvation

Terence M. O'Keeffe

A puzzle has been presented in the recent past in Northern Ireland: what is the correct description of the person who dies as a result of a hunger-strike? For many the simple answer is that such a person commits sui-cide, in that his is surely a case of "self-inflicted death."[1] Where then is the puzzle? It is that a number of people do not see such deaths as sui-cides. I am not here referring to political propagandists or paramilitaries, for whom the correct description of such deaths is "murder by Mrs. Thatch-er" or "killed by British intransigence" (to quote advertisements in the Belfast nationalist press at the time of Bobby Sands's death). I am rather thinking of some theologians who, despite being opposed to the hunger-strike and indeed publicly condemning the whole campaign, refused to describe what the hunger-strikers did as suicide.

Trying to understand the reasoning involved in this judgment will force us to clarify our notion of what is to count as suicide, the role of the intention of the person acting in such a way as to bring about his own death, and through this notion, something about the principle of 'double effect' which seems to be invoked by theologians in cases like

From *Philosophy* 56 (1981): 349–63. Copyright © Royal Institute of Philosophy. Reprinted with the permission of Cambridge University Press.

this. The following reflections however exclude any consideration of the *politics* of hunger-striking in Northern Ireland, which would require a very different treatment. (Whether it will be possible to exclude entirely any political judgment from a description of the deaths of hunger-strikers will perhaps be clearer by the end of the discussion.)

I have pointed out that there are some people who wish to deny the suicide verdict on the deaths of hunger-strikers. It is clear why they wish to do so. They hold the view that suicide or self-killing is always an extremely grave sin, and if this were the correct description of the hunger-striker, many difficulties would be raised for the pastoral care of such persons, especially their right to be admitted to the sacraments and to the last rites.

Perhaps I should indicate the source of their moral disapproval of suicide, for clearly it is not a verdict shared by all. For some people, there is no more difficulty about the suicide verdict on hunger-strikers than there is about a similar verdict on Socrates, the Christian martyrs, the death of Christ himself, Captain Oates, deaths of heroic self-sacrifice such as the soldier who throws himself on a live grenade in order to shield his comrades, etc. There will be no difficulty about accepting a suicide verdict in these sorts of cases because there is in their minds no *moral* disapproval implied by the term "suicide." Disapproval will only arise in cases where it could be suggested that it is not *rational* to end one's life. The officer who chooses "death rather than dishonor" when exposed as an embezzler of the mess funds and shoots himself, could be said to be acting irrationally in supposing that "dishonor"—i.e., living on after quitting the army in disgrace, with one's reputation destroyed, etc.—is somehow necessarily worse or necessarily less desirable than no life at all. David Hume, in "On Suicide," suggests that it is a proper course of action for those leading a life "loaded with pain and sickness, with shame and poverty." Whatever the propriety of escaping through suicide from intolerable pain and suffering, it is not immediately obvious why a life of shame and poverty is not rationally to be preferred to no life at all.

This form of rational calculation of the merits or demerits of suicide depends on a thesis, which I will call the *humanist* thesis, which is roughly this: that I am the judge of my best interests and that I am in charge of my life. It is a thesis about the moral autonomy of the rational individual. Thus, the decision to end my own life, provided it is taken as a fully human decision, on rational grounds, unclouded by irrational fears and motives, is for me and for me alone to make. Richard Brandt provides a good account of the sort of reasoning one might expect:

> [It] is a choice between future world-courses: the world-course which includes my demise, say, in an hour from now, and several possible ones which contain my demise at a later point. . . . The problem, I take it, is to decide whether the expected utility to me of some possible world-course in which I go on for another twenty years is greater than or less than the expectable utility to me of the one in which my life stops in an hour. . . . We compare the suicide world-course with the continued-life world-course (or several of them) and note the features with respect to which they differ. We then assign numbers to these features, representing their utility to us if they happen, and then multiplying this utility by a number which represents the probability that this feature will occur. . . . The world-course with the highest sum is the one that is rationally chosen.[2]

Brandt goes on to argue that "there is a close analogy between the analysis of the rationality of suicide and a firm's analysis of the rationality of declaring bankruptcy and going out of business."[3]

Such reasoning about suicide, based on the humanist thesis, is very different from the moral reasoning of those who wish to condemn suicide as an extremely evil act. The essential difference is to be found in their contention that one's life is *not* one's own to end or take away. Roy Holland is surely right in calling this standpoint "religious" and in seeing it as based on some thesis about life as a *gift*.The thesis can be expressed in different ways. Aquinas expresses it as follows: "Life is God's gift to man and is subject to his power. . . . Whosoever takes his own life sins against God even as he who kills another's slave sins against that slave's master. It belongs to God alone to pronounce sentence of life and death" (*Summa Theologica* IIa IIae, q.64, a.5). This echoes Socrates' verdict in the *Phaedo*: "Mortals are the chattels of the gods. . . . Wouldn't you be angry if one of your chattels should kill itself when you had not indicated that you wanted it to die?" (62B). The "slaves and chattels" imagery can give way to more "martial" allusions. So Locke argues in the *Second Treatise on Civil Government* that "everyone is bound to preserve himself and not to quit his station willfully" (ch. 2). And Kant argues in similar vein in the *Lectures on Ethics:* "A suicide . . . arrives in the other world as one who has deserted his post . . . as a rebel against God. . . . Human beings are sentinels on earth and may not leave their posts unless relieved by another beneficent hand."

It is true that other reasons are advanced in this tradition to establish the sinfulness of suicide. Aquinas gives two others. Suicide is a sin against oneself, thus violating a "natural law" of self-love. And it is a sin against the community and hence a form of injustice, appealing here to a principle that "every part as such belongs to the whole." But neither of these arguments carries the same weight as the "life as a gift" thesis. It is on this that the religious condemnation of suicide rests most strongly.

This condemnation of suicide does not appear to have been central to Christian teaching from the beginning. It is only with Augustine that Christian thinkers begin to specify suicide as the most evil of sins. There are a number of suicides in the Old Testament: Samson, who brought the temple crashing down upon himself with the cry, "May I die with the Philistines" (Judg. 16, 30); Abimelech, who ordered his sword-bearer to kill him when he was mortally wounded by a stone dropped by a woman "So that no one may say of me: a woman killed him" (Judg. 9, 53); Saul, who said "Draw your sword. I do not want uncircumcised men to gloat over me" and, when his sword-bearer refused, fell upon his own sword (2 Sam. 31, 4); and Ahithophel, who is perhaps the clearest case of suicide in the Old Testament: on having his advice rejected by Absalom, he retired to his home village and "having set his house in order, strangled himself and so died" (2 Sam. 17, 23). Yet these acts were not commented on particularly adversely by early writers. The suicide of the "archcriminal" Judas Iscariot is recorded in the Gospel of Saint Matthew without comment—almost, indeed, as a measure of his repentance. It is only later writers who see in Judas's suicide the real reason for his damnation. Tertullian appears to have had no difficulty in describing the death of Jesus as suicide (because he voluntarily gave up his life). What spurred Augustine and others to condemn suicide was the suicidal mania of many of the early Christian martyrs, and in particular the sect of the Donatists, for whom, taking the high valuation of martyrdom seriously, the most sensible course after baptism was to preserve the state of grace thus gained by instant death, by martyrdom if possible but by suicide if necessary. It was in opposition to this that Augustine stressed the condemnation of suicide as a frustration of God's plan and a rejection of God in rejecting his gift of life. Only in the sixth century did Church law incorporate a ban on suicide. Until that time, the promise of escape from temptation and the guarantee of posthumous glory were powerful inducements to martyrdom *and* to suicide.

Despite these caveats, it is clear that after this time a universal condemnation of suicide forms part of the Christian tradition, basing itself on several arguments. Suicide is a type of murder—self-murder—and thus shares the general condemnation of homicide. It is this that gives Aquinas his first argument against suicide, that it is a sin against oneself. It is also seen as an act which in a certain sense forestalls God's will for us. If death is the final evil and the last crucial test for the believer, it is because it signifies our ultimate helplessness before God. Suicide expresses a fundamental refusal of trust in God. It is a quitting of our station before we have been relieved, a desertion to the enemy. Most centrally, however, the thesis about life as a gift brings out clearly something about the religious person's vision of the human relationship with God. It is seen as one of dependence on a divine order of things and thus as a rejection of the total autonomy of the human individual. This sense of dependence is comparable to that sense of *contingency* about the world, that feeling of creaturehood and dependence, that provides the context for causal arguments for the existence of God. Just as, in its absence, some philosophers cannot see the point of such argumentation and, like Hume, find it senseless to "go one step beyond this mundane system" to seek a cause and explanation of the world's existence, so without the essentially religious context of "life as a gift," suicide can appear as a rational option. The humanist outlook is guided by some such principle as that in general life is to be preferred to nonlife. But this can yield to prudential considerations in favor of suicide (and of other cases of killing—euthanasia, abortion, infanticide for grossly handicapped infants, etc.). The other view, which insists on transcending the notion of human autonomy and on seeing a meaning in life beyond this world, insists that life is not one's own. One who ends his own life is thus guilty of denying the religious meaning of life itself. It is in this way that it can be seen as one of the very worst of sins. Holland quotes G. K. Chesterton's *Orthodoxy*: "The man who kills a man, kills a man. The man who kills himself, kills all men; as far as he is concerned he wipes out the whole world."[4] Suicide is thus seen as a turning of one's back on God, a deliberate spurning of God's gift, and ultimately a spurning of God himself. For Chesterton, it is "the refusal to take an interest in existence, the refusal to take the oath of loyalty to life."[5] Thus it is not just a narrowly religious sin; it is also a metaphysical sin. For Schopenhauer, suicide is not to be seen as an escape from the will or from the world, though it might appear so. It is in fact a strong *assertion* of the will: "Just because the suicide cannot cease to will, he ceases to live; and the will affirms itself here even through the abolition of one of its own phenomena because it can no more affirm itself otherwise."[6] Even where life is regarded as painful, the metaphysical duty is to endure, to retain that "first loyalty to things" (to quote Chesterton again).[7] Life as a gift is not necessarily to be understood as meaning that life is always something pleasant or desirable. Within this "religious" tradition, it can also appear as a trial and a burden. The notion of gift underlines that it is given to us and that we hold it in trust, whether to enjoy or not. A. Phillips Griffiths pinpoints the meaning of the act of suicide as it is seen within the "life as a gift" thesis:

> Suicide is the paradigm of evil, the "elementary" sin. To seek death is to reject life (or if it is not, is it really suicide?) and this is fundamentally different from other futile bad strivings of a particular will. . . . In all other sinning we fail to accept the world whatever it is—we would not have it as it is. In suicide we would not have it at all. We desire not merely a different meaning but no meaning: no God.[8]

If I wish to comment on the debate concerning the moral judgment on the hunger-striker—whether he commits suicide or not—I must take for granted this religious perspective. Otherwise the judgment could only be based on the question whether it is ever a rational thing to do to give up your life for a cause. In the eyes of many people it is a rational choice in certain circumstances. And if one asks whether on pragmatic grounds it is justifiable, then clearly it has been a useful tool in political struggles in the past in Ireland and elsewhere. (One can think not only of the death by hunger-strike of Terence McSweeny in the 20s, which had an enormous political impact, but even more recently in the early 70s a determined hunger-strike by prisoners like Billy McKee achieved political status for I.R.A. and loyalist prisoners.)

So I wish to pose the question of the suicide verdict on hunger-striking against the religious view which sees suicide as always a gravely evil act. What is to count within this tradition as an act of suicide? With the "life as a gift" thesis, *any* taking of life is problematic (including war, capital punishment, killing in self-defense, etc.). In the case of suicide, it is self-killing that is evil. There are many clear candidates for acts which could be described as self-killings—cutting one's own throat, poisoning oneself, throwing oneself in front of a train. But there are examples (one is given by Roger Frey)[9] where, though the killing is done by another person, it was so arranged by the person who dies that it seems more natural to call it an act of suicide than homicide. To commit a "self-killing" then, it is not necessary that one kills oneself or that one dies by one's own hand. Whether one shoots oneself or so arranges things that one is shot by someone else, it would still count as suicide. Again, in certain cases, refusing to act or refraining from acting would seem to count more as suicide than anything else. The person who has swallowed poison, however unwittingly, but who refuses to save his life by taking a simple antidote—would we not count him as much a suicide as the person who swallows poison to kill himself?

Can we then say that to commit suicide is by a negative or positive action or by so arranging the circumstances to put one's life in danger and die as a result? I hardly think that this would do. The person who attempts to cross the Place de la Concorde on foot would commit suicide not only in the humorous sense but in the morally blameworthy sense. Many accidental actions which cause our deaths would then have to be counted as suicides. We have to add something to the effect that the agent is aware of the possible results of his action. With the addition of this "subjective" factor—knowing the likely results of one's action—we have an account of suicide that we can call the *objective* account—in fact we have Durkheim's description: "The term suicide is applied to all cases of death resulting directly or indirectly from a positive or negative action of the victim himself which he knows will produce this result."[10]

This account specifically excludes from the definition of suicide any reference to motives, intentions, or reasons for taking the action. Durkheim wishes to exclude these in order to give a sociological account of suicide. His definition then will include a number of actions which have commonly, in the religious tradition we are talking about, been excluded as examples of suicide: martyrs going knowingly to their deaths, soldiers acting heroically and dying to save others, self-sacrifices, etc. Now this is of no significance for Durkheim since he did not wish the description of an action as suicide to have any *moral* connotation whatever. But for the religious tradition, suicide is always a gravely evil action. So some way has to be found of distinguishing such evil acts from acts in which a person knowingly goes to his death, is capable of avoiding it, does not act to save his own life, and yet is not to be counted a suicide and morally condemned. I am not so much thinking of examples like those given by Saint Jerome who, though asserting that it was never permissible to kill oneself to avoid persecution and torture, nevertheless conceded that it was permissible for a virgin to take her own life when her chastity was threatened; rather more of straightforward cases of martyrdom and those deaths commonly called sacrificial deaths.

Consider the case of Fr. Maximilian Kolbe who, during the last war, substituted himself in the condemned cell for a fellow prisoner (a Jewish father of a family) and was executed. Did Kolbe commit suicide? If not, on what grounds do we rule out such deaths as suicides? Would we not be inclined to say that, in order to commit suicide, one must not only knowingly and willingly go to one's death, not act to save oneself, be capable of avoiding it—above all, one must *want* to die? The case of Fr. Kolbe, and the much discussed case of Captain Oates, are not suicides because they did not *intend* their deaths but rather some other state of affairs—the saving of the Jewish father, the lives of the other members of Scott's expedition.

In other words, the intention to die is the crucial factor in distinguishing suicides from those cases of deaths. To intend to terminate one's own life—this is the distinguishing mark of the act of suicide. To bring about the termination of one's life by so arranging the circumstances that one dies but with the intention of bringing about some other state of affairs, is not suicide. So the person who leaps from the boat, intending to kill himself and succeeding, commits suicide. The person who leaps from the boat, which is hopelessly overcrowded and in danger of sinking with the children, into a shark-infested sea does not commit suicide because he does not intend to die but rather to lighten the boat. The notion of the agent's intention seems neatly to distinguish the two cases and to enable us to withhold the moral condemnation in the description of the latter act—not suicide but self-sacrifice, a clear case of "laying down one's life for one's friends" which demands our moral approval.

Another way of discriminating between these types of cases is offered by Roy Holland.[11] Holland, too, wishes to condemn suicide for roughly the reasons I have picked out as the religious view. Equally he approves of the sort of action taken by Captain Oates and refuses the description of it as a suicide. He draws a number of distinctions between what Oates did—walking out of the tent into a blizzard and finally dying—and what he might have done but did not do—kill himself. Had Oates stepped outside the tent and shot himself, then according to Holland he would have committed suicide. But it is not what he did but what he *allowed to happen* to him that counts. Oates did not *do* anything, he let it be done to him, a difference then between *doing* and *suffering*. His action (walking from the tent) only indirectly led to his death, whereas had he cut his throat, that would have directly led to his death. The "temporal lapse" between his action of walking from the tent and his death seems significant to Holland. And so, too, does Oates's use of "natural phenomena" (the blizzard, the intense cold, etc.) rather than a gun or a knife. And in general Holland appeals to what he calls "the context and spirit" of Oates's action which makes it possible to say that Oates was no suicide but a self-sacrificing and heroic individual.

Can we use these three accounts of suicide to comment on the deaths by hunger-strike? Under the "objective" or nonintentional label, the only factor which becomes significant is whether the hunger-striker can be said to *know* that his action will lead to his death. If he does, then he is a suicide. A lot will depend on what one wants to put into the term 'know' here. Obviously in one sense, a person embarking on a hunger strike *knows* that he will die after a (variable) period without taking food (normally somewhere between 40 and 75 days). It would, however, be argued that, since his decision is to continue on the hunger-strike until the government yields to his demands and since he does not know whether or when the government will give in, then in *some* sense he does not know whether he will die or not. But of course in this sense almost every suicide does not know that the act will be successful—he may be rescued and revived in time, he may only wound and not kill himself, etc. The point seems too slender to serve as an exoneration of the hunger-striker from the suicide verdict. (We must remember that the point of this account was to remove any moral condemnation from the description anyway.) And finally, since this account included both positive and negative actions, there seems little to be gained by attempting to say that the hunger-striker does not *do* anything to kill himself (such as cutting his throat) but simply does nothing in refusing food.

Holland's account at first sight looks a more promising candidate for those who wish to deny the suicide description to the hunger-striker. After all, a number of the features of the Oates case are directly paralleled in the case of the hunger-striker. Hunger-striking is arguably a "suffering" rather than a "doing." The prisoner *does* nothing, he "allows" the lack of food to kill him, he "suffers" death rather than inflicts it upon himself. His death is thus not the direct result of his action but indirect, just as Oates's was. There is a temporal lapse between the decision to undertake the hunger-strike and death itself. The hunger-striker uses a "natural phenomenon" of hunger like Oates. And finally it is surely plausible that the "context and spirit" of the hunger-strike, which has to be seen within the political struggle in Northen Ireland, is a context quite different from our ordinary understanding of suicides.

Now here, unlike the case of the 'objective' account, there is something at stake. Holland wants to use his analysis of suicide to *acquit* Oates of the charge of suicide, which is morally blameworthy. Could we similarly acquit the hunger-striker? The trouble is, I think, that examined individually, the various discriminating features suggested by Holland may not do their job. Take the doing-suffering distinction. In the sense that Oates places himself in a position where he will surely die, he encompasses his own death, he so arranges it that he dies. I cannot see that this is not a case of "doing." Holland will not allow that the man who places his head on the railway line could be said simply to allow the train to crush him, thus suffering death rather than doing something like cutting his throat. Nor that the man who drowns himself could equally claim that he was merely "letting the water kill him." But why not? In the latter case, we have *all* Holland's features—indirectness, lapse of time, natural phenomenon. And the appeal to the "spirit and context" of the event looks like no more than a decision that we are not going to count certain cases as suicides. It does not seem to me that Holland's analysis is the most profitable line to take for those seeking to acquit the hunger-striker.

Surely, it might be argued, just what is missing from the debate is a clear reference to the *intention* of the hunger-striker. The intention of Oates was not to end his life but to save his companions. The intention of Fr. Kolbe was to save the Jewish father. The intention of the soldier who throws himself on the grenade is to save the lives of his comrades. And the intention of the hunger-striker is to put pressure on the government to accede to his demands. The suicide simply intends his death— by shooting himself, drowning himself, by not acting to save himself from life-threatening circumstances, by so arranging the circumstances that his death is brought about. And this is what distinguishes suicide from these cases of heroic self-sacrifice or legitimate protest.

But this is not sufficient. In Oates's case, he must surely be held to intend his death in *some* sense. If he did not knowingly and intentionally go to his *death,* he would not have accomplished his purpose: if his companions thought that he might survive, they would perhaps have risked their lives to go out and search for him. It is only his death that absolves them from this obligation. In a real sense, Oates intended to terminate his life. Similarly, Kolbe intended to go to execution in the other's place, he must have intended to present himself for execution—otherwise he would not have succeeded in his purpose. Must not the hunger-striker, too, in-tend his death—particularly if, as in present circumstances, the first death did not cause the government to waver? (It appears that the hunger-strik-ers were prepared to have three or four die before they hoped for vic-tory.) And the hunger-striker who, before lapsing into a coma, instructs his family not to have him revived by medical intervention—surely he must in some sense intend his death as further pressure on the government.

But suppose we accept that in these cases they all in some sense in-tend to die but that this is secondary to their primary intention—saving lives, pressuring the government, etc. They perhaps accept that they will die, thus intending it in this sense, but their overriding intention is other-wise; for we can have actions with multiple intentions. It is the overrid-ing intention which gives the act its moral character. In the cases of self-sacrifice, the overriding intention is clearly not to die but to save others—borne out by the fact that, if there had been any *other* way of saving them, the act would not have been performed. We might consider that, because these deaths were in some sense not ends in themselves but instru-mental in achieving other ends and purposes, they are not to be counted suicides. This would permit us to define suicide as a self-killing in which the overriding intention is simply to end one's life and there is no fur-ther independent objective involved in the action. Let us call such self-killings *noninstrumental* in order to distinguish them from *instrumental* self-killings where the acts are performed for some other purposes such as heroism, the salvation of others, political protest, or whatever.[12]

This is an attractive thesis. It allows us clearly to distinguish the cases of Oates, Kolbe, and others—all instrumental self-killings—from the true cases of suicide. The hunger-striker, too, is clearly acquitted of the suicide verdict since his is an instrumental self-killing, undertaken for the pur-pose of political protest or whatever. Notice, however, that we now have to include in our definition of nonsuicidal self-killings all sorts of cases. The Buddhist monk who burns himself to death in front of the American Embassy is not a suicide. The person who shoots himself on learning that he is incurably ill in order to save his family from the pain and trouble of looking after him is not a suicide. Anyone who acts to bring about his own death for *any* reason other than that of simply bringing about his own death is not a suicide.

I am prepared to accept these self-killings as nonsuicidal, but many people who invoke the intention of the agent to discriminate between sui-cide and nonsuicide would be unhappy with these cases. Let me quote what a Maynooth theologian, Denis O'Callaghan, wrote in the *Irish Times* *à propos* the present hunger-strike: "The suicide verdict turns on a fact—does the hunger-striker intend his death (as the Czech student Jan Palach did when he burned himself to death in protest against the Russian invasion of his country) or is he prepared to accept death possibly as the inevitable side-effect of a protest action on which he has embarked?" Clearly the implication is that, while Jan Palach necessarily intended his death (even though his is a case of instrumental self-killing) and hence committed suicide, the hunger-striker *may* be described as not intending his death at all but merely accepting it as an unintended side-effect of the protest.

What I take to be implied here is the principle of double effect as it has been invoked by Catholic theologians, particularly though by no means exclusively in cases involving the killing of others, especially in abortions. There has been an enormous amount of discussion of this principle and of the sorts of cases to which the principle claims to apply. I am thinking not only of the classic cases from obstetric practice (as treated by Philippa Foot and Jonathan Bennett)[13] but all those complicated examples in the recent literature: the "trolley problem" where Edward is on a runaway railway trolley whose brakes have failed and who can only steer the trolley so as to kill five people on the main line or one person on a branch line; the potholers trapped in the cave with water rising and the only exit blocked by a fat man, where the alternative to drowning for the party is to blow the fat man out of the hole with dynamite; the miraculous health pebble floating towards the island where the only alternative is to direct it to one beach saving thereby five lives or another where it will save only one.[14]

The principle of double effect is primarily about acts and their effects, and not primarily about agents' intentions, as is sometimes asserted. The principle can be stated roughly as follows: when an agent is faced with an action which he foresees has two effects, one good and other evil, he may perform the action under the following conditions:

1. The action must itself be a good action or at least morally neutral;

2. The performance of the action must bring about at least as much good as evil;

3. The evil effect must not be a means to achieving the good effect;

4. The agent must have a justifying and sufficient reason for acting rather than refraining from acting.

That the action must not itself be an evil action is clearly demanded by the context of the whole principle—a morality where there are certain actions which are absolutely forbidden. Thus we cannot suppose that we can perform *any* morally evil act no matter what the good which will come about. Within this tradition direct killing of an innocent person may never be justified. The second condition requires that the good and evil consequences must be at least balanced. The principle could not be invoked in cases where an act leads to a trivial good and a great evil. The third condition merely states that the end can never justify the means. We are not therefore discussing doing evil acts which have good results, but rather acts which are morally permissible where the good resulting is coterminous with the evil, or, we might say, at least as immediate. Finally, the fourth condition makes it clear that it is only in rare cases, where we have serious and morally convincing reasons for acting rather than not acting, that the principle can be invoked.

Now one of the points I want to bring out in this account of the double effect principle is that, though I believe it to be an adequate account, it has not brought into the reckoning the *intention* of the agent. It is true of course that, if the agent is permitted to do the action by the principle, he must not intend the evil consequences but only the good. But this intention is not the morally specifying feature of the action. It is not simply because he can exclude from his intention the evil consequences of the act that the act is permissible. Rather it is because it is an act of a certain sort—good or at least morally neutral, with two effects, etc.—that he is permitted to perform it, and of course we can add that in its performance he must not will the evil.

Let me construct a story to try to bring this point out. A submarine with a full crew of 125 men is holed under water in the forward section. If a certain bulkhead door is not closed immediately, the submarine will lose its buoyancy and will sink, making rescue impossible because of the depth, and all will be lost. Behind the bulkhead door are five crewmen who will certainly be killed by drowning should the door be closed. The captain may act to close the door according to the principle of double effect. Why? The act—closing the bulkhead door—is not evil in itself, rather morally neutral. Clearly the good effect (saving 120 men) is not outweighed by the evil effect. Nor is the good effect achieved by means of the evil effect. The proof of this is that the door would still be closed even if the men were not there. It is not their *deaths* that save the other men. And clearly the captain has a morally justifying reason for acting rather than doing nothing. Notice that the captain's *intention* is not really all that relevant—we need not talk about his only intending the good and excluding from his intention the evil effects to permit the action. Of course he must not intend their deaths or take pleasure in their suffering (for example, in the case where one of the five has been his wife's lover). But it is not *this* which makes the act permissible.

Compare this story with another in which the principle would not apply. The submarine is holed on the bottom but is awaiting rescue. Unfortunately air is running out and, in order to save the majority of the crew, the captain shoots five crew members and disposes of their bodies through torpedo tubes. This would I think violate the principle in a number of ways. The act—shooting them—would be held to be directly evil, thus contradicting the first condition. Even though the good results would outweigh the evil, as in our first story, the third condition would be violated. It is by their *deaths* that he brings about the good effect (sufficient air for the rest). The proof is that unless the five die—that is, stop breathing—the good effect cannot come about. So despite having a good reason for acting, he must refrain from shooting them. What he cannot do, I think, is say: I am shooting them but of course I do not intend their deaths, only the saving of the others.

Let me apply this interpretation of the principle of double effect to the case of the potholers and the fat man. We could argue that blowing the fat man to pieces is directly killing him and therefore is ruled out as a candidate for the act of double effect—since it violates our first condition. The act is not morally neutral or good; as a direct killing, it is evil. This is why, in abortion cases, provided we view the fetus as a fully human person, operations like craniotomy (crushing the skull of the fetus and removing it) cannot be justified by the principle of double effect—they are held to be direct killings of the innocent and therefore absolutely wrong, regardless of the doctor's intention, or the good which will result.

I do not of course wish to exclude intention from the description of the act. The acts themselves—closing the bulkhead door, shooting the crew members, blowing up the fat man, etc.—must of course be voluntary intentional acts in order to be candidates for the principle of double effect. What I am saying is that the principle is concerned about the *act which is intended*—how it can be described, its effects, etc.—and not, as is commonly thought, about the *intention of the act* itself.

But notice what we have to take for granted here. In the abortion case, it is presupposed that the act of killing the fetus is intrinsically evil while the act of letting the mother die is not. In the potholing example, we must make a similar judgment. But could it be argued that we have in both these cases an act—performing an operation, causing an explosion—which has two effects, one good and the other evil, and that the act itself is morally neutral? It is here that the principle of double effect as I have outlined it gets confused with a quite different set of problems, those of describing an action—what proximate effects are to be counted as part of the description of the action itself (I did not kill him, I only moved my hand with a knife in it)? What moral difference is there between positive and negative actions, between acting and refraining, between killing and letting die? All these have been receiving considerable attention in the literature and I content myself with merely referring to them.[15] (Clearly Catholic theology tries to draw a distinction between craniotomy [direct killing] and hysterectomy of a diseased womb which contains a living fetus [indirect killing] on some such grounds.) What I am saying is that the principle of double effect is misstated if it is held to differentiate between acts on the agent's intention alone.

Incidentally this is the source of the worry that Anscombe has about the principle of double effect, when she asserts that the denial of the principle has been the corruption of non-Catholic thought and its abuse the corruption of Catholic thought.[16] The notion of the agent's intention which could be "directed" like a searchlight, on to the good effect but missing out the bad effects, she suggests, owes a lot to Cartesian psychology, with the intention viewed as an interior state of mind which could be produced at will.

Thus I find that O'Callaghan's attempt to distinguish the hunger-striker (not intending his death but merely accepting it as a necessary consequence, an inevitable side-effect of his action) from the case of Jan Palach (who directly intends his death) begs too many questions. I would prefer to define suicide as the act of a person who noninstrumentally intends his death, and allow all instrumental self-killings to evade the verdict on suicide. After all, in the religious tradition we are presupposing as background, what makes the suicide that most evil of persons is that he simply wants to turn his back on life, to reject the gift of life whatever happens.

We could devise a sort of post-mortem verification of this. Suppose that the dead person is miraculously revived for an instant after death. What would his reaction be? The "true" suicide, the noninstrumental self-killer, will ask to be put back to death, so to speak—he literally does not wish to continue living. The self-sacrificer—Oates, Kolbe—would not react in this way at all. They would be delighted with revivification. (They would of course ask whether their actions had their desired effect—were the others saved? And they might say that they were prepared to do it again if necessary. But their *deaths* were not what they wanted.) The hunger-striker is perhaps a slightly different case. He would presumably ask—did the government give in? If the demands had been granted, then there would be no question of "redying." If not? Well, the very determined person would not say—put me back to death. He would say—I shall begin another hunger-strike unless the government. . . . And it is this difference which makes him not a case of the "true" suicide.

Thus, I would say that the real act of suicide is noninstrumental self-killing in which the horror, for the religious person, of the rejection of God's gift and indeed of God himself are manifest. I recognize that the religious sin of suicide becomes, on this definition, an almost inconceivable act. The suicide is the person who kills himself for no other reason than to terminate his life. His motives must be curious—a sort of black, "religious" pessimism, arising from a hatred of self, of the world, of *existence* itself, which is presented as a total and final rejection of meaning and of God. (The desire for annihilation is difficult for the person who believes in an immortal soul or in an afterlife—because such a person believes that you *cannot* actually end your existence. I can only suggest that such is the rejection of God by this true anti-theist that he must be seen as saying: I reject existence utterly and I destroy deliberately, out of a sort of disgust at life, all that I can destroy—my bodily existence.) Such a suicide seeks an end to self-hood out of disgust at existence. Another conceivable motivation is that of a suicide who kills himself as the ultimate act of egotism, the final and irrevocable act of freedom in which he asserts his ego against the world and against even a nonexistent god. So Kirillov, in Dostoyevsky's *The Devils,* shoots himself as an act of self-will: "I cannot understand how an atheist could know that there is no god and not kill himself at once. . . . I am bound to shoot myself because the most important point of my self-will is to kill myself. . . . I am killing myself to show my defiance and my new terrible freedom." Out of these barely conceivable cases, we can begin to discern the depth of the religious condemnation of suicide as the worst and most ultimate of sins.

These are of course extremely *rare* cases—almost all the acts which are commonly called "suicide" are not of this type at all. Most are what I am calling instrumental self-killings. We must remember however that this does not of itself mean that they are all morally permissible. Clearly, within the 'life as a gift' thesis, one can only put one's life at risk for a grave and justifying cause, for a morally worthy cause. Oates and Kolbe did so in order to save others at the expense of their own lives. The moral judgment on the hunger-striker we have been considering may not turn on the suicide question, but it does turn on the morally worthy cause, on the grave and serious reasons for acting in this way. My personal opinion is that the recent hunger-strike was never justified within that religious tradition. To back up this judgment would require a consideration of the political and military struggle in Northern Ireland at the present time, and the detailed reasons for the hunger-strike—and a very different paper.[17]

NOTES

1. The medical certificates were amended to record the cause of death as "starvation," after protests by the families of the dead hunger-strikers at the original pathologist's report which recorded "self-imposed starvation." The coroner found that the cause of death was "starvation, self-imposed."

2. Richard Brandt, "The Morality and Rationality of Suicide," in *Moral Problems,* J. Rachels (ed.). (New York: Harper and Row, 1971), pp. 375–76 [see this volume, chapter 15, p. 193].

3. Ibid., p. 376 [see chapter 15].

4. R. F. Holland, "Suicide," in *Talk of God* (Royal Institute of Philosophy Lectures, volume 2, 1967–68), p. 82.

5. G. K. Chesterton, *Orthodoxy* (London: Sheed and Ward, 1939), p. 115.

6. Schopenhauer, *The World as Will and Representation,* section 69.

7. Chesterton, (note 5), p. 119.

8. A. Phillips Griffiths, "Wittgenstein, Schopenhauer, and Ethics," in *Understanding Wittgenstein* (Royal Institute of Philosophy Lectures, volume 7, 1974), p. 112.

9. R. G. Frey, "Suicide and Self-Inflicted Death," in *Philosophy* 56 (1981): 193–202 [see this volume, chapter 9].

10. Emile Durkheim, *Suicide: A Study in Sociology* (London: Routledge and Kegan Paul, 1952), pp. 41–42.

11. Holland, (note 4), pp. 89–91.

12. This is the definition of suicide given by Joseph Margolis in "Suicide," in *Ethical Issues in Death and Dying,* T. L. Beauchamp and S. Perlin (eds.). (Englewood Cliffs, N.J.: Prentice-Hall, 1978), pp. 92–97. Margolis wishes to distinguish the case of the person who rationally and noninstrumentally wishes to end his life from cases where the person acts irrationally (e.g., mental illness) or instrumentally (e.g., self-sacrificing deaths).

13. Philippa Foot, "The Problem of Abortion and the Doctrine of the Double Effect," in *The Oxford Review* 5 (1967); Jonathan Bennett, "Whatever the Consequences," in *Analysis* 26 (1966).

14. E.g., Judith Jarvis Thomson, "Killing, Letting Die and the Trolley Problem," in *The Monist* 59 (1976); R. A. Duff, "Intentionally Killing the Innocent," in *Analysis* 33 (1973).

15. E.g., Daniel Dinello, "On Killing and Letting Die," in *Analysis* 31 (1971); Bruce Russell, "On the Relative Strictness of Negative and Positive Duties," in *American Philosophical Quarterly* 14 (1977).

16. G. E. M. Anscombe, "War and Murder," in *Nuclear War and Christian Conscience,* Walter Stein (ed.). (London: Merlin Press, 1961), p. 50.

17. This paper was first read to the Philosophy Staff Seminar at the University of Warwick, and a revised version to the Staff Seminar at the New University of Ulster. I am grateful for the helpful discussion and criticism I received.

11

Mastering the Concept of Suicide

Glenn C. Graber

All of us mastered the use of the concept of suicide in the course of learning our native language. We know that certain deaths are appropriately classified as suicides (for example, the deaths of Romeo, Juliet, Ernest Hemingway), whereas certain others are clearly not suicides (for example, the deaths of John F. Kennedy, Lyndon Johnson).* The difficulty comes when we try to classify them as we do.

WHAT IS SUICIDE?

Let us consider some cases that result in death in different ways:

Reprinted by permission of the University of Tennessee Press. Glenn C. Graber's "The Rationality of Suicide" from *Suicide and Euthanasia: The Rights of Personhood*, eds. Samuel E. Wallace and Albin Eser. Copyright © 1981 by The University of Tennessee Press.

    * There are, of course, some borderline cases in which we are unsure, even after all the facts are clear, whether to call a death suicide (several such cases are noted below). An advantage of the technique of analysis employed herein is that it allows us to make use of the insights we gain from examining clear cases to decide whether these borderline cases are appropriately classified as suicides.

A. Arnold is fired from his job, the only job for which his training and his interests equip him. Upon returning home to tell his wife, whom he loves dearly, he finds a note saying that she has left him for another man—in fact, the very man who has just been given his former job. As he lights the stove to fix himself a lonely dinner, it explodes and his expensive home burns to the ground—which reminds him that he has allowed the fire insurance to lapse. After thinking through his plight for several hours, he takes a pistol (the only item that survived the fire) and blows his brains out.

B. Bernice is whisting a merry tune as she washes dishes, but when she touches the switch to turn on the garbage disposal, she is electrocuted and dies.

C. Clyde has a song in his heart as he eats his breakfast, but when he takes a sip of his coffee (into which his wife has mixed a generous amount of strychnine), he slumps over dead.

Case *A* clearly is a case of suicide. Cases *B* and *C,* just as clearly, are not. What precisely is the difference between them?

The reply that first comes to mind is to say that Arnold killed himself by his own action, whereas Bernice and Clyde were killed by somebody or something other than themselves. The trouble is that there is a wholly reasonable sense in which Bernice and Clyde can be said to have killed themselves by their own actions, too. After all, Bernice reached out her hand and touched the switch. The electricity did not come to her. (Contrast the case of someone struck by lightning.) And Clyde picked up the cup and drank from it. (Contrast someone who is held down and has poison injected into his veins.) Thus, the fact that one's death results from one's own action is not sufficient to qualify it as suicide. Some cases of accidental death (Bernice) and murder (Clyde) also have this feature.

What we need is to find some feature of the cases that distinguishes Arnold's action in relation to his death from the actions of Bernice and Clyde. One possibility is the difference between characteristic effects and unusual or uncharacteristic effects. This criterion would distinguish the cases cited so far in the proper way. To put a gun to one's temple and pull the trigger (as Arnold did) or to remain in a closed room in which gas is escaping as someone we will call Donna—Case *D*—did, characteristically causes death. In contrast, to put a cup of coffee to one's lips and drink does not characteristically cause death. It is only in the unusual circumstance in which there is poison in the coffee that a drink of it will kill. Bernice's death is likewise an uncharacteristic effect of her action, for it is only when something has gone wrong with the wiring (which is not the usual condition) that it will be a fatal act to touch a wall switch.

However, this criterion will not serve to distinguish suicide from other kinds of death in all cases. It is possible to commit suicide by means of abnormal or uncharacteristic conditions if we know about them in advance. If one knows, for example, that there is a short in a particular wall switch, then one could commit suicide by stepping into a bucket of water and then touching the switch. If Clyde had watched his wife pour the poison into his coffee and knew that it was poison but deliberately drank it anyway, we would judge that he committed suicide. In these cases, death is an uncharacteristic result of the action, but it is a suicide nevertheless. Hence we cannot define suicide in these terms.

These counterexamples suggest another possibility. Perhaps knowledge is the key to the distinction between suicide and other kinds of deaths. At least one theorist has thought so. The sociologist Emile Durkheim defined suicide as "all cases of death resulting directly or indirectly from a positive or negative act of the victim himself, which he knows will produce this result."[1]

This definition does not seem adequate. It does not distinguish between the following two cases, the first of which seems clearly to be suicide and the second of which seems equally clearly not to be.

E. Edgar is a wartime secret agent who is captured by the enemy. Knowing that he will be tortured mercilessly to the death, he takes a cyanide capsule from a hidden compartment in his shoe, bites into it, and dies.

F. Francine is another wartime secret agent who is captured. She has heard before about these particular captors and knows that they always torture to the death any agent who refuses to divulge the information they are after. Nevertheless, she refuses to tell them anything. After three painful days, she dies from their tortures.

The difference between these two cases is a subtle one, but since it is both real and important to the analysis of suicide, we will take time here to bring the difference into focus. In order to do this, we must note some preliminary points about the nature of action.

A single action has multiple effects. For example, Edgar's action not only has the consequence of bringing about his death but has the additional effects of guaranteeing that he does not divulge whatever strategic information he knows ("Dead men tell no tales") and of sparing him the pain of tortures that would otherwise be inflicted upon him. It may have still other effects as well. If we suppose (as is not unlikely) that one of Edgar's captors had been assigned the responsibility of searching captured agents in order to find concealed poisons and if the commanding officer is as ruthless as his procedures for treatment of captives suggest that he is, then Edgar's action of taking the poison may have the additional consequence of prompting the execution of one of his captors.

Some effects are causally independent of other effects. For example, consider the two consequences: Edgar's guaranteeing the protection of his secrets and his bringing about the execution of his captor who failed to find the poison. Neither of these is directly causally related to the other. The captor is executed, not because the secrets were successfully protected but because he failed to carry out an assigned responsibility. Imagine that Edgar had not succeeded in guaranteeing the protection of his secrets. Imagine, for example, that he had inadvertently left a written statement of them intact in his pocket. The chances are good that his captor would still have been executed. The fact that the soldier had failed to do his assigned duty would remain as a basis for punishment. Thus these two consequences are both effects of Edgar's swallowing the poison, but they are causally independent of each other.

Now we must consider the element of intention in action. Some of the effects of a given action are intended. More specifically, whatever goals the agent hoped or planned to achieve by performing the action are intended effects of the action. It is reasonable to assume that both Edgar and Francine had the same ultimate goal in mind in doing what they did; both wanted to protect the secret information in their possession. Thus this is clearly an intended effect of their respective actions. In addition, it is likely that Edgar was also influenced by the realization that death from the poison would spare him the pain of torture. Hence this can plausibly be interpreted as a second, coordinate goal of his action and thus another intended effect of it.

Some effects of an action are not intended effects. Consider the consequence of the execution of one of Edgar's captors who failed to find the concealed poison. Surely this was not an intended effect, and Edgar was probably not even aware of it. Of course, it is possible that he did know beyond reasonable doubt what would happen. Even if he knew, however, it would still seem a mistake to say that he intended for it to happen. Awareness of this consequence played no role at all in his decision to act as he did. His interest was in protecting his secret information in the best way he knew. The realization that an enemy soldier would die as a result of his action made him neither more nor less inclined to act. The consequence was, then, a by-product, a side-effect, or an incidental effect of his action, perhaps foreseen but not intended. This brings us to our final point about action: some of the effects of an action that are foreseen are nevertheless not intended effects.

It is important to establish this last point because it provides the key to the distinction between Edgar and Francine and, ultimately, the basis for criticism of Durkheim's definition of suicide. For Francine, her own death was a by-product or a side-effect of her action and not an intended effect. Her goal was to protect her secret information in the best way she knew—by remaining silent. She would have done the same thing if she had not known what her captors would do to her as a result or if she had known that they would *not* kill her, and her realization that these particular captors would surely kill her made her neither more nor less inclined to talk. (This may be too strong. She may have been tempted to talk in order to save her life, but she resisted the temptation and remained silent.) Thus her death was a foreseen but unintended consequence of her action.

Edgar's situation is importantly different from this. His death was not a side-effect of his action. Rather it was a part of the means he used to achieve the goal. His taking the poison caused his death, which in turn provided the guarantee that his secret information would be protected (assuming now that he remembered to destroy any notes).

The upshot of all this is that knowledge of the consequences is not what distinguishes suicide from nonsuicide, as Durkheim believed. Both Edgar and Francine knew that they were going to die. What makes the difference between suicide and nonsuicide is the intention of the agent. Edgar intended to die, and thus his death was suicide. Francine, in contrast, did not intend to die. Her death was a side-effect of her action, and thus she was not a suicide.

Now we have the key to the proper analysis of suicide. The crucial difference between suicide and other kinds of death is to be found in the intentions or purposes of the person who dies. This can be seen clearly in the cases discussed so far. Arnold, Donna, and Edgar (our three suicides) all did what they did with the express intention of bringing about their own deaths. Bernice, Clyde, and Francine, in contrast, had no such intention. Bernice was trying to get rid of the garbage. Clyde wanted to drink some coffee. Francine was interested in protecting the national security of her country. None of the nonsuicides acted with the intention of dying; all of the suicides did act as they did for this purpose.

Thus our suggestion passes the first test of adequacy for a proposed analysis. It matches our preanalytic judgment about what is suicide and what is not. The crucial difference between suicide and other kinds of death is to be found in the intentions or purposes of the person who dies.

However, there is still some work to be done. In the first place, we need to formulate the suggestion into an explicit analysis so that we can see more clearly precisely what it involves. One way of doing this is proposed by Joseph Margolis, who defines suicide as "the deliberate taking of one's life in order simply to end it, not instrumentally for any ulterior purpose."[2] This description might fit the cases of Arnold and Donna. If someone had asked them, just prior to their acts, why they were preparing to take their lives, each might have answered by saying something like "My life is meaningless; I simply want to end it." This is the sort of thing Margolis has in mind.

However, Margolis's definition does not fit Case E—Edgar. If we had asked Edgar whether his purpose in taking the poison was simply to bring about his own death, he would undoubtedly have answered with a resounding "No!" He had two ulterior purposes: to protect his secrets and to prevent the pain of torture. If he could have found any way to reach these goals that did not involve his death, he would not have ended his life. For him death was a means or instrument to an ulterior purpose, not something he wanted in itself. And yet we have agreed that his death was suicide. Hence Margolis's proposal for a definition of suicide must be rejected, since it does not match our practical classifications in this sort of case.

Indeed, there is a plausible aspect in the cases of Arnold and Donna that would put even them outside Margolis's analysis. Suppose they explained their actions by saying, "I am in despair, and I want to end this awful anguish." The natural interpretation of this is to say that ending their anguish is for them an ulterior purpose to which their deaths are means or instruments. Then, on Margolis's analysis of suicide, we would have to say that these deaths are not suicides. Surely this is mistaken.

R. B. Brandt works intention into the analysis of suicide in a more promising way. He proposes the following definition:

> "Suicide" is conveniently defined, for our purposes, as doing something which results in one's death, either from the intention of ending one's life or the intention to bring about some other state of affairs (such as relief from pain) which one thinks it certain or highly probable can be achieved only by means of death or will produce death.[3]

However, this analysis is too broad. By this definition, not only would Edgar's death qualify as suicide, but so would Francine's. Her goal is to protect her nation's secrets, but she is aware that it is highly probable that the same action that will achieve this purpose (that is, her negative action of remaining silent) will also produce her death, since it is the known practice of her captors to kill agents who remain silent. Yet we agreed earlier that Francine's death is not a suicide. Thus we cannot be satisfied with Brandt's definition as it stands. It is too close to Durkheim's definition.

We can produce an accurate analysis of suicide by amending Brandt's definition. It will not do simply to drop the whole phrase that reads: "or the intention to bring about some other state of affairs (such as relief from pain) which one thinks it certain or highly probable can be achieved only by means of death or will produce death." What would be left is equivalent to Margolis's definition, which we have already discarded as too narrow.

The analysis of suicide we want must include deaths (like Edgar's) that are intentionally brought about as a means to some ulterior purpose, and it must exclude deaths (like Francine's) that are foreseen but not intended consequences of deliberate actions. Actually, we can achieve this quite easily. All we have to do is to drop the last four words of Brandt's analysis: "or will produce death." It is this phrase that brings in deaths that are foreseen side-effects of deliberate actions.

Incorporating into Brandt's definition the two changes we have made, we get the following analysis of suicide: suicide is defined as doing something that results in one's death in the way that was planned, either from the intention of ending one's life or the intention to bring about some other state of affairs (such as relief from pain) that one thinks it certain or highly probable can be achieved only by means of death.

Let us test this analysis further by examining its implications for certain additional cases. First consider this pair of cases:

G. Gary is in constant and intense pain caused by terminal cancer. Somehow he manages to get hold of a large quantity of a pain-killing drug, which he takes all at once, saying "I want to die. It is the only way to get rid of this awful pain."

H. Helen's physical condition is just like Gary's. She takes the same amount of the same drug, but she says, "It is not my intent to die. I am taking this dosage because nothing less will completely relieve the pain and I am determined to get rid of the pain, even if it results in my death."

Our analysis compels us to say that Gary's death is suicide, but Helen's is not. (This assumes, as we must in the absence of explicit evidence to the contrary, that they both mean exactly what they say. The ultimate goal of the action in both cases is to be rid of pain. For Gary death is a means to this end, but for Helen death is a by-product of the means chosen (which is to take a dosage large enough to guarantee that it is effective in relieving the pain). There is another way of specifying the difference between these two cases. Helen might not be disappointed if she were to wake up a day or two later to find that the pain had returned. Not dying is compatible with (although not dictated by) her expressed motive that all she wants is temporary relief from the pain, a rest for a while from the burden. Gary, however, would react differently. If he were to come out of a coma a day or two later and still be racked with pain, he would be bound to feel that he had failed to accomplish his purpose.

There is one more implication of this analysis that should be brought to attention. We have said that the classification of an act as suicide hinges on the person's intentions or purposes. Psychologists tell us, however, that many people who attempt suicide do not really want to die. Their actions are really desperate calls for help from other people. Of course, some of them take a stronger action than they had intended, or the intervention they had expected does not come, and they do die. By our analysis, these are not actually suicides. They are accidental deaths. Thus our definition entails that what police agencies and others regard as the clear-cut cases of suicide may not be suicides at all. Just because someone is found hanging from a rope he tied around his own neck or dead from a self-administered dose of sleeping pills, this does not prove that he committed suicide. It may not have been his intention to die.

SUICIDE AND RATIONALITY

Is suicide ever rationally justified? It seems clear that it sometimes is. Let us begin with a closer look at the situation of our old friend Edgar, the wartime secret agent.

His only choice is between death today and death tomorrow after incalculable pain, and surely he is correct in choosing the former option. It is the only rational decision in such a situation. Think first about his appraisal of the facts of the situation. He has reliable evidence that it is the practice of these captors to kill captured agents. He would be hoping against hope if he expected his captors suddenly to become soft-hearted and spare his life. It would be equally unrealistic for him to think that his compatriots would risk the success of their cause (as well as their own lives) to rescue him. He must face the fact: he is doomed.

Now consider his appraisal of the values. It would also be irrational not to want to avoid torture. The pain of it is reason enough to want to avoid it, but Edgar must also consider the very real risk that he might break under torture and betray his cause.

We acknowledge the rational justification of suicide in this sort of case, whether in fiction or in real life. Our usual emotional reaction is admiration for the agent for having the courage to follow what is obviously the only sensible course of action. (Note that we have not said he is morally justified. This is still an open question that we will consider shortly.)

Let us now step back from this example and see if any general principles can be abstracted from it. The way to get at such a principle is to ask, what is it about Edgar's situation that leads us to think that it is rationally justified for him to take his life? The answer to this question seems obvious. Once we are convinced that Edgar has not made any errors in his appraisal of either facts or values in the situation (which is one important aspect of rationality, but not the whole story), what persuades us of the correctness of his decision to kill himself is our own perception that he is better off dead. If we measure the advantages and disadvantages of both options open to him, it appears clear that the choice to kill himself immediately is likely to produce a greater total value (or, what amounts to the same thing, a lesser total disvalue) than the other option. This, then, is our general principle of rational justification in suicide. *It is rationally justified to kill oneself when a reasonable appraisal of the situation reveals that one is really better off dead.*

The best way to see whether the principle really works in practice is to try to apply it to some specific cases. Let us look, for example, at the situations of the cancer patients Gary and Helen. Each of them is racked with pain from an incurable and terminal illness. Gary decides to kill himself, and Helen chooses a course of action that results in her death. Are their decisions rationally justified? Only a short period of life is left to them anyway, and it will be filled with extreme pain. In this respect, their situations parallel Edgar's. It would be unreasonable of them to expect a sudden spontaneous remission of the disease at this advanced stage or to expect a miracle cure in the near future. There are some additional values open to them that are not available to Edgar. Whereas Edgar has only his hostile captors to keep him company, Gary and Helen are surrounded by more or less sympathetic people—including their families and close friends. The value of these contacts cannot be ignored, and their decisions would be unjustified if they left these values out of account altogether. Surely Gary and Helen are not being unreasonable, however, if they question whether the continuation of these human contacts is worth the cost in pain. The value of the benefits of which immediate death would rob them is outweighed by the disvalue of the pain from which death would spare them. Hence we must say that they would be better off dead and that ending their lives is therefore rationally justified.

Several points about this argument call for comment. First, the judgment that a certain person would be better off dead must be made entirely from that person's own point of view. The fact that Gary is an emotional and financial burden to his family is, in itself, totally irrelevant to the issue of whether he would be better off dead. It might be significant in saying that the family would be better off if he were dead, but that is another matter entirely. Of course, if Gary is aware that he is a burden, this awareness will be detrimental to his welfare. Awareness of being a burden, however, is different from the fact of being a burden, and only the former counts toward saying that he would be better off dead.

The second point is more complicated—and more controversial. We must acknowledge a person's own tastes and preferences, but we must not extend a blanket acceptance of all the value judgments of that person. If, for example, a woman prefers chocolate ice cream to pistachio, we cannot say she is mistaken, but if she prefers eating mud pies to eating ice cream, then surely she *is* mistaken about values. Objective values set the limits for legitimate and reasonable preferences. Among things that are of roughly equivalent value (for example, ice cream of different flavors, foods of different kinds of roughly equal nutritional value, styles of music, literature, or art), the choice between them is left entirely to the individual's taste, but if the value that the person places upon a thing (for example, mud pies) is too far out of line with its objective value, then the preference is labeled as unreasonable.

This principle is not limited in application only to trivial matters. The same value governs the choice of an occupation and a lifestyle. The choice between a career as a lawyer and one as a teacher is largely a matter of individual taste, but it would be unreasonable (economic considerations aside) for one to devote one's whole life to collecting odd bits of string.

The same reasoning applies in the case of Gary. We may feel that if we were in Gary's situation, we would rather endure the pain in order to be able to continue to enjoy association with other human beings. Nevertheless, if Gary himself is not afraid of death (with the resulting loss of human contacts) and prefers it to a continuation of the pain, we have no right to impose our preferences upon him by insisting that he is not rationally justified in ending his life. On the other hand, if Gary were to say that he saw no value at all in human associations or no disvalue at all in death, he would be mistaken and we ought not to endorse his mistaken judgment.

In other sorts of cases, it is much more difficult to form a judgment about the rationality of suicide. Let us look at one troublesome case:

I. Irene used to be an especially active young woman. She was a professional dancer, and all her favorite avocations were strenuous physical activities like swimming and tennis. As the result of an automobile accident, she is now paralyzed from the waist down, and the functioning of her arms and hands is impaired. She decides to kill herself, saying, "I would be better off dead than living as an invalid."

Is her decision rationally justified?

It must be admitted that she faces something less than a full and complete life. She will never again be able to participate in the kinds of physical activities that mean so much to her (and also mean a great deal to many other people). Her life is diminished as a result of her accident. We acknowledge this when we speak of the accident as a misfortune or a tragedy and of its results as a loss.

However, a life thus diminished is not totally robbed of value. Irene still has a lot going for her. She has full use of her mental faculties, full ability to communicate, and partial mobility of arms and hands. She can maintain meaningful and satisfying relationships with other people, and if she put her mind to it, she could undoubtedly devise a number of projects within her capabilities with which to occupy her time. We all know of people who have managed to make satisfying lives for themselves in spite of handicaps even more severe than Irene's.

There is no guarantee that Irene will make a satisfying life for herself. We all also know of persons, some less severely handicapped than Irene, who have remained bitter about their losses and, as a result, have isolated themselves from others and refused to try to devise constructive ways to fill their time. It is hardly surprising to find that many of these people look back over their lives and judge that they would have been better off dead. A life of bitterness, isolation, and self-pity is not clearly superior to no life at all.

In the face of these conflicting possibilities, how are we to determine whether Irene's life is worth continuing? It is tempting to say that the judgment should be left entirely up to Irene. However, this is an evasion. Unless we are willing to aid her by constructing a set of rational criteria on which she can make her judgment, we will have done nothing but add the weight of responsibility to her already considerable burdens. Moreover, it is an open question whether she is in a better position to apply such criteria than is somebody else.

Another tempting response is to look to capabilities rather than to possibilities or probabilities as the basis for evaluating life prospects. We have said, for example, that Irene can maintain relationships and that she could devise projects. Whether she actually does any of these things is, presumably, up to her, but even if she fails to do them, the fact remains that she is capable of doing them. This might seem to be enough by itself to say that her prospective life is worth living.

The trouble is that it may not be within Irene's power to control whether she fulfills these capabilities. She may fight against bitterness only to find that she cannot prevent its setting in. She may actively try to devise projects to fill her time only to discover that she cannot develop an interest in any of them. How one reacts to a misfortune like Irene's is not decided by conscious choice or effort of will. It involves factors in the personality that have developed gradually over the whole of one's life and cannot be altered in any direct way. Irene's entire life has been oriented exclusively toward physical activities, and so she may not have any interest in or ability for the kind of quiet activities that are now her only hope. If she finds that these activities fail to satisfy her no matter how hard she tries to develop an interest in them, it would be neither surprising nor unreasonable for her to conclude that she would be better off dead.

There is one very important value that we have not yet considered in Irene's situation. In order to get at it, let us look at the following case.

J. Jeremy is yet another secret agent who is captured, but his captors are very different from those who got hold of Edgar and Francine. Instead of brutal torture, these people go in for subtle and sophisticated techniques of brainwashing that render the subjects willing and eager to share any strategic information they happen to know. Jeremy knows of their methods, and he also knows (as a result of a battery of psychological tests that were taken in the course of his training) that he is highly susceptible to such influence. He bites a cyanide capsule because he does not want to become the sort of person who would willingly betray his cause.

What this case brings out is the value of personal ideals and personal integrity. Jeremy has set certain ideals for the kind of person he wants to be; among other things, he wants to be loyal to his country. Departure from this ideal might not cause him any pain. If the brainwashing is totally effective, he might not feel any pangs of conscience when he betrays his country. He might even be proud of doing so because after the brainwashing is completed, he will have become a different kind of person than he is now—the kind whose loyalties are directed toward the cause of his captors. The trouble is that he does not now want to become the kind of person he would then be.

This is what is so insidious and frightening about techniques of brainwashing. They affect what is most dear to the victim. They alter one's ideals for the kind of person one wants to be and thus violate personal integrity. In an important sense, they destroy the *person* and put a different person in its place.

Irene might view her prospects in a way parallel to Jeremy's line of thought. She might be fairly sure that, in time, she could adjust to life as an invalid and find satisfaction in it. She can remember that she has enjoyed short periods in bed with minor illnesses, and she can imagine

herself becoming totally engrossed in television soap operas, syrupy nov-
els, and needlework. She also realizes that she finds a certain amount
of pleasure in the pity and solicitude of those who come into contact
with her, and she can imagine that this aspect of her nature will expand
as time goes on.

However, she does not want to become this sort of person. She has
always regarded this part of her nature as unworthy and has worked to
suppress it, and the prospect of its becoming dominant in her personality
is repugnant to her. She would rather end her life than to become this
sort of person.

SOME GENERAL CONCLUSIONS

In the course of this discussion, we have reached some general conclusions
about the rationality of suicide. It might be helpful to repeat them in
a list here:

1. Some suicides are rationally justified (Edgar and Gary, for example).

2. Some suicides are not rationally justified.

3. It is rationally justified to kill oneself if a reasonable appraisal of
    the situation reveals that one is really better off dead. This is the
    criterion of rational justification for suicides.

4. The judgment that a certain person is (or is not) better off dead
    should be justified exclusively:
    a. From the person's own point of view;
    b. Within limits, on the basis of the person's own tastes and
        preferences;
    c. On the basis of actual preferences (present and future), rather
        than abstract capabilities.

5. The prospective suicide's judgment of whether he or she would
    be better off dead is not the last word on the matter. The person
    may be mistaken.
    a. The person may make a wrong prediction about the degree
        to which his or her present values are likely to be satisfied.
        ("I'll never be able to keep up my career now that I am
        blind.")

    b. The person may make a wrong prediction about the nature of his or her future values. ("I'll never learn to enjoy the kind of activities open to me now that I am confined to a wheelchair.")

    c. The person may have mistaken values.

6. In judging whether a person would be better off dead, we must take into account not only the person's present and future values but also his or her personal ideals and personal integrity (Jeremy, for example).

NOTES

1. *Suicide,* trans. Spaulding and Simpson (Glencoe, Ill.: The Free Press, 1951), p. 44.

2. *Negativities: The Limits of Life* (Columbus: Charles E. Merrill Publishing Co., 1975), p. 26.

3. "The Morality and Rationality of Suicide," in *A Handbook for the Study of Suicide,* ed. Seymour Perlin (New York: Oxford University Press, 1975), p. 363 [see chapter 15 in this volume].

Part Three

Is Suicide Moral?
Is It Rational?

12

Preventing Suicide

Edwin S. Shneidman

In almost every case of suicide, there are hints of the act to come, and physicians and nurses are in a special position to pick up the hints and to prevent the act. They come into contact, in many different settings, with many human beings at especially stressful times in their lives.

A suicide is an especially unhappy event for helping personnel. Although one can, in part, train and inure oneself to deal with the sick and even the dying patient, the abruptness and needlessness of a suicidal act leaves the nurse, the physician, and other survivors with many unanswered questions, many deeply troubling thoughts and feelings.

Currently, the major bottleneck in suicide prevention is not remediation, for there are fairly well-known and effective treatment procedures for many types of suicidal states; rather it is in diagnosis and identification.[1]

Reprinted from the *American Journal of Nursing* (May 1965), 65:111-16, with the permission of the publisher. Copyright © 1965 by the American Journal of Nursing Company. All rights reserved.

153

ASSUMPTIONS

A few straightforward assumptions are necessary in suicide prevention. Some of them:

Individuals who are intent on killing themselves still wish very much to be rescued or to have their deaths prevented. Suicide prevention consists essentially in recognizing that the potential victim is "in balance" between his wishes to live and his wishes to die, then throwing one's efforts on the side of life.

Suicide prevention depends on the active and forthright behavior of the potential rescuer.

Most individuals who are about to commit suicide are acutely conscious of their intention to do so. They may, of course, be very secretive and not communicate their intentions directly. On the other hand, the suicidally inclined person may actually be unaware of his own lethal potentialities, but nonetheless may give many indirect hints of his unconscious intentions.

Practically all suicidal behaviors stem from a sense of isolation and from feelings of some intolerable emotion on the part of the victim. By and large, suicide is an act to stop an intolerable existence. But each individual defines "intolerable" in his own way. Difficulties, stresses, or disappointments that might be easy for one individual to handle might very well be intolerable for someone else—in *his* frame of mind. In order to anticipate and prevent suicide one must understand what "intolerable" means to the other person. Thus, any "precipitating cause"—being neglected, fearing or having cancer (the fear and actuality can be equally lethal), feeling helpless or hopeless, feeling "boxed-in"—may be intolerable for *that* person.

Although committing suicide is certainly an all-or-none action, thinking about the act ahead of time is a complicated, undecided, internal debate. Many a black-or-white action is taken on a barely pass vote. Professor Henry Murray of Harvard University has written that "a personality is a full Congress" of the mind. In preventing suicide, one looks for any indications in the individual representing the dark side of his internal life-and-death debate. We are so often surprised at "unexpected" suicides because we fail to take into account just this principle that the suicidal action is a decision resulting from an internal debate of many voices, some for life and some for death. Thus we hear all sorts of postmortem statements like "He seemed in good spirits" or "He was looking forward to some event next week," not recognizing that these, in themselves, represent only one aspect of the total picture.

In almost every case, there are precursors to suicide, which are called "prodromal clues." In the "psychological autopsies" that have been done at the Suicide Prevention Center in Los Angeles—in which, by interview with survivors of questionable accident or suicide deaths, they attempt to reconstruct the intention of the deceased in relation to death—it was found that very few suicides occur without casting some shadows before them. The concept of prodromal clues for suicide is certainly an old idea; it is really not very different from what Robert Burton, over 300 years ago in 1652, in his famous *Anatomy of Melancholy,* called "the prognostics of melancholy, or signs of things to come." These prodromal clues typically exist for a few days to some weeks before the actual suicide. Recognition of these clues is a necessary first step to lifesaving.

Suicide prevention is like fire prevention. It is not the main mission of any hospital, nursing home, or other institution, but it is the minimum ever-present peripheral responsibility of each professional; and when the minimal signs of possible fire or suicide are seen, then there are no excuses for holding back on lifesaving measures. The difference between fire prevention and suicide prevention is that the prodromal clues for fire prevention have become an acceptable part of our commonsense folk knowledge; we must also make the clues for suicide a part of our general knowledge.

CLUES TO POTENTIAL SUICIDE

In general, the prodromal clues to suicide may be classified in terms of four broad types: verbal, behavioral, situational, and syndromatic.

Verbal

Among the verbal clues we can distinguish between the direct and the indirect. Examples of direct verbal communications would be such statements as "I'm going to commit suicide," "If such and such happens, I'll kill myself," "I'm going to end it all," "I want to die," and so on. Examples of indirect verbal communications would be such statements as "Goodbye," "Farewell," "I've had it," "I can't stand it any longer," "It's too much to put up with," "You'd be better off without me," and, in general, any statements that mirror the individual's intention to stop his intolerable existence.

Some indirect verbal communications can be somewhat more subtle. We all know that in human communication, our words tell only part of the story, and often the main "message" has to be decoded. Every parent or spouse learns to decode the language of loved ones and to understand what they really mean. In a similar vein, many presuicidal communications have to be decoded. An example might be a patient who says to a nurse who is leaving on her vacation, "Goodbye, Miss Jones, I won't be here when you come back." If some time afterward she, knowing that the patient is not scheduled to be transferred or discharged prior to her return, thinks about that conversation, she might do well to telephone her hospital.

Other examples are such statements as "I won't be around much longer for you to put up with," "This is the last shot you'll ever give me," or "This is the last time I'll ever be here," a statement which reflects the patient's private knowledge of his decision to kill himself. Another example is, "How does one leave her body to the medical school?" The latter should never be answered with factual information until after one has found out why the question is being asked, and whose body is being talked about. Individuals often ask for suicide-prevention information for a "friend" or "relative" when they are actually inquiring about themselves.

Behavioral

Among the behavioral clues, we can distinguish the direct and the indirect. The clearest examples of direct behavioral communications of the intention to kill oneself is a "practice run," an actual suicide attempt of whatever seriousness. Any action which uses instruments which are conventionally associated with suicide (such as razors, ropes, pills, and the like), regardless of whether or not it could have any lethal outcome, must be interpreted as a direct behavioral "cry for help" and an indication that the person is putting us on our alert. Often, the nonlethal suicide attempt is meant to communicate deeper suicidal intentions. By and large, suicide attempts must be taken seriously as indications of personal crisis and of more severe suicide potentiality.

In general, indirect behavioral communications are such actions as taking a lengthy trip or putting affairs into order. Thus the making of a will under certain peculiar and special circumstances can be an indirect clue to suicidal intention. Buying a casket at the time of another's funeral should always be inquired after most carefully and, if necessary, prompt action (like hospitalization) taken. Giving away prized possessions like a watch, earrings, golf clubs, or heirlooms should be looked on as a possible prodromal clue to suicide.

Situational

On occasion the situation itself cries out for attention, especially when there is a variety of stresses. For example, when a patient is extremely anxious about surgery, or when he has been notified that he has a malignancy, when he is scheduled for mutilative surgery, when he is frightened by hospitalization itself, or when outside factors (like family discord, for example, or finances) are a problem—all these are situational. If the doctor or nurse is sensitive to the fact that the situation constitutes a "psychological emergency" for that patient, then he is in a key position to perform lifesaving work. His actions might take the form of sympathetic conversation, or special surveillance of that patient by keeping him with some specially assigned person, or by requesting consultation, or by moving him so that he does not have access to windows at lethal heights. At the least, the nurse should make notations of her behavioral observations in the chart.

To be a suicide diagnostician, one must combine separate symptoms and recognize *and label* a suicidal syndrome in a situation where no one symptom by itself would necessarily lead one to think of a possible suicide.

In this [essay] we shall highlight syndromatic clues for suicide in a medical and surgical hospital setting, although these clues may also be used in other settings. First, it can be said that patient status is stressful for many persons. Everyone who has ever been a patient knows the fantasies of anxiety, fear, and regression that are attendant on illness or surgery. For some in the patient role (especially in a hospital), as the outer world recedes, the fantasy life becomes more active; conflicts and inadequacies and fears may then begin to play a larger and disproportionate role. The point for suicide prevention is that one must try to be aware especially of those patients who are prone to be psychologically overreactive and, being so, are more apt to explode irrationally into suicidal behavior.

Syndromatic

What are the syndromes—the constellations of symptoms—for suicide? Labels for four of them could be: depressed, disoriented, defiant, and dependent-dissatisfied.

1. Depressed: The syndrome of depression is, by and large, made up of symptoms which reflect the shifting of the individual's psychological interests from aspects of his interpersonal life to aspects of his private psychological life, to some intrapsychic crisis within himself. For example, the individual is less interested in food, he loses his appetite, and thus loses weight. Or, his regular patterns of sleeping and waking become disrupted, so that he suffers from lack of energy in the daytime and then sleeplessness and early awakening. The habitual or regular patterns of social and sexual responses also tend to change, and the individual loses interest in others. His rate or pace or speed of talking, walking, and doing the activities of his everyday life slows down. At the same time, there is increased preoccupation with internal (intrapsychic) conflicts and problems. The individual is withdrawn, apathetic, apprehensive and anxious, often "blue" and even tearful, somewhat unreachable and seemingly uncaring.

Depression can be seen too in an individual's decreased willingness to communicate. Talking comes harder, there are fewer spontaneous remarks, answers are shorter or even monosyllabic, the facial expressions are less lively, the posture is more drooped, gestures are less animated, the gait is less springy, and the individual's mind seems occupied and elsewhere.

An additional symptom of the syndrome of depression is detachment, or withdrawing from life. This might be evidenced by behavior which would reflect attitudes, such as "I don't care," "What does it matter," "It's no use anyway." If an individual feels helpless he is certainly frightened, although he may fight for some control or safety; but if he feels hopeless, then the heart is out of him, and life is a burden, and he is only a spectator to a dreary life which does not involve him.

First aid in suicide prevention is directed to counteracting the individual's feelings of hopelessness. Robert E. Litman, chief psychiatrist of the Los Angeles Suicide Prevention Center, has said that "psychological support is transmitted by firm and hopeful attitude. We convey the impression that the problem which seems to the patient to be overwhelming, dominating his entire personality, and completely insidious, is commonplace and quite familiar to us and we have seen many people make a complete recovery. Hope is a commodity of which we have plenty and we dispense it freely."[2]

It is of course pointless to say "Cheer up" to a depressed person, inasmuch as the problem is that he simply cannot. On the other hand, the effectiveness of the "self-fulfilling prophecy" should never be overestimated. Often an integral part of anyone's climb out of a depression is his faith and the faith of individuals around him that he is going to make it. Just as hopelessness breeds hopelessness, hope—to some extent—breeds hope.

Oftentimes, the syndrome of depression does not seem especially difficult to diagnose. What may be more difficult—and very much related to suicide—is the apparent improvement after a severe depression, when the individual's pace of speech and action picks up a little. The tendency then is for everyone to think that he is cured and to relax vigilance. In reality the situation may be much more dangerous; the individual now has the psychic energy with which to kill himself that he may not have had when he was in the depths of his depression. By far, most suicides relating to depression occur within a short period (a few days to 3 months) after the individual has made an apparent turn for the better. A good rule is that any significant change in behavior, even if it looks like improvement, should be assessed as a possible prodromal index for suicide.

Although depression is the most important single prodromal syndrome for suicide—occurring to some degree in approximately one-third of all suicides—it is not the only one.

2. Disoriented: Disoriented people are apt to be delusional or hallucinatory, and the suicidal danger is that they may respond to commands or voices or experiences that other people cannot share. When a disoriented person expresses any suicidal notions, it is important to take him as a most serious suicidal risk, for he may be in constant danger of taking his own life, not only to cut out those parts of himself that he finds intolerable, but also to respond to the commands of hallucinated voices to kill himself. What makes such a person potentially explosive and particularly hard to predict is that the trigger mechanism may depend on a crazed thought, a hallucinated command, or a fleeting intense fear within a delusional system.

Disoriented states may be clearly organic, such as delirium tremens, certain toxic states, certain drug withdrawal states. Individuals with chronic brain syndromes and cerebral arteriosclerosis* may become disoriented.

---

*Hardening of the arteries—Ed.

On the other hand, there is the whole spectrum of schizophrenic and schizoaffective disorders, in which the role of organic factors is neither clearly established nor completely accepted. Nonetheless, professional personnel should especially note individuals who manifest some degree of nocturnal disorientation, but who have relative diurnal lucidity. Those physicians who see the patients only during the daytime are apt to miss these cases, particularly if they do not read nurses' notes.

Suicides in general hospitals have occurred among nonpsychiatric patients with subtle organic syndromes, especially those in which symptoms of disorientation are manifested. One should look, too, for the presence of bizarre behavior, fear of death, and clouding of the patient's understanding and awareness. The nurse might well be especially alert to any general hospital patient who has any previous neuropsychiatric history, especially where there are the signs of an acute brain syndrome. Although dyspnea* is not a symptom in the syndrome related to disorientation, the presence of severe dyspnea, especially if it is unimproved by treatment in the hospital, has been found to correlate with suicide in hospitals.

When an individual is labeled psychotic, he is almost always disoriented in one sphere or another. Even if he knows where he is and what the date is, he may be off base about who he is, especially if one asks him more or less "philosophic" questions, like "What is the meaning of life?" His thinking processes will seem peculiar, and the words of his speech will have some special or idiosyncratic characteristics. In general, whether or not such patients are transferred to psychiatric wards or psychiatric hospitals, they should—in terms of suicide prevention—be given special care and surveillance, including consultation. Special physical arrangements should be made for them, such as removal of access to operable screens and windows, removal of objects of self-destruction, and the like.

3. Defiant: The Welsh poet, Dylan Thomas, wrote: "Do not go gentle into that good night/. . . . rage, rage against the dying of the light." Many of us remember, usually from high school literature, Henley's "Invictus," "I am master of my fate/ I am the captain of my soul." The point is that many individuals, no matter how miserable their circumstances or how painful their lives, attempt to retain some shred of control over their own fate. Thus a man dying of cancer may, rather than passively capitulate to the disease, choose to play one last active role in his own life by picking the time of his death; so that even in a terminal state (when the staff

---

*Shortness of breath—Ed.

may believe that he doesn't have the energy to get out of bed), he lifts a heavy window and throws himself out to his death. In this sense, he is willful or defiant.

This kind of individual is an "implementer."[3] Such a person is described as one who has an active need to control his environment. Typically, he would never be fired from any job; he would quit. In a hospital he would attempt to control his environment by refusing some treatments, demanding others, requesting changes, insisting on privileges, and indulging in many other activities indicating some inner need to direct and control his life situation. These individuals are often seen as having low frustration tolerance, being fairly set and rigid in their ways, being somewhat arbitrary and, in general, showing a great oversensitivity to outside control. The last is probably a reflection of their own inability to handle their inner stresses.

Certainly, not every individual who poses ward-management problems needs to be seen as suicidal, but what personnel should look for is the somewhat agitated concern of a patient with controlling his own fate. Suicide is one way of "calling the shot." The nurse can play a lifesaving role with such a person by recognizing his psychological problems and by enduring his controlling (and irritating) behavior—indeed, by being the willing target of his berating or demanding behavior and thus permitting him to expend his energies in this way, rather than in suicidal activities. Her willingness to be a permissible target for these feelings and, more, her sympathetic behavior in giving attention and reassurance even in the face of difficult behavior are in the tradition of the nurturing nurse, even though this can be a difficult role continually to fulfill.

4. Dependent-dissatisfied: Imagine being married to someone on whom you are deeply emotionally dependent, in a situation in which you are terribly dissatisfied with your being dependent. It would be in many ways like being "painted into a corner"—there is no place to go.

This is the pattern we have labeled "dependent-dissatisfied."[4] Such an individual is very dependent on the hospital, realizing he is ill and depending on the hospital to help him; however, he is dissatisfied with being dependent and comes to feel that the hospital is not giving him the help he thinks he needs. Such patients become increasingly tense and depressed, with frequent expressions of guilt and inadequacy. They have emotional disturbances in relation to their illnesses and to their hospital care. Like the "implementer," they make demands and have great need for attention and reassurance. They have a number of somatic complaints, as well as complaints about the hospital. They threaten to leave the hospital against medical advice. They ask to see the doctor, the chaplain, the chief nurse. They request additional therapies of various kinds. They make statements like, "Nothing is being done for me" or "The doctors think I am making this up."

The reactions of irritability on the part of busy staff are not too surprising in view of the difficult behavior of such patients. Tensions in these patients may go up especially at the time of pending discharge from the hospital. Suicide prevention by hospital staff consists of responding to the emotional needs and giving emotional support to these individuals. With such patients the patience of Job is required. Any suicide threats or attempts on the part of such patients, no matter how "mild" or attention-getting, should be taken seriously. Their demand for attention may lead them to suicide. Hospital staff can often, by instituting some sort of new treatment procedure or medication, give this type of patient temporary relief or a feeling of improvement. But most of all, the sympathetic recognition on the part of hospital staff that the complaining, demanding, exasperating behavior of the dependent-dissatisfied patient is an expression of his own inner feelings of desperation may be the best route to preventing his suicide.

CO-WORKERS, FAMILY, FRIENDS

Suicide is "democratic." It touches both patients and staff, unlettered and educated, rich and poor—almost proportionately. As for sex ratio, the statistics are interesting: Most studies have shown that in Western countries more men than women commit suicide, but a recent study indicates that in certain kinds of hospital settings like neuropsychiatric hospitals, a proportionately larger percentage of women kill themselves.[5] The information in this [essay] is meant to apply not only to patients, but to colleagues, and even to members of our families as well. The point is that only by being free to see the possibility of suicidal potential in everybody can suicide prevention of anybody really become effective.

In our society, we are especially loath to suspect suicide in individuals of some stature or status. For example, of the physicians who commit suicide, some could easily be saved if they would be treated (hospitalized, for example) like ordinary citizens in distress. Needless to say, the point of view that appropriate treatment might cause him professional embarrassment should never be invoked in such a way so as to risk a life being lost.

In general, we should not "run scared" about suicide. In the last analysis, suicides are, fortunately, infrequent events. On the other hand, if we have even unclear suspicions of suicidal potential in another person, we do well to have "the courage of our own confusions" and take the appropriate steps.'

These appropriate steps may include notifying others, obtaining consultation, alerting those concerned with the potentially suicidal person (including relatives and friends), getting the person to a sanctuary in a psychiatric ward or hospital. Certainly, we don't want to holler "Fire" unnecessarily, but we should be able to interpret the clues, erring, if necessary, on the "liberal" side. We may feel chagrined if we turn in a false alarm, but we would feel very much worse if we were too timid to pull that switch that might have prevented a real tragedy.

Earlier in this [essay] the role of the potential rescuer was mentioned. One implication of this is that professionals must be aware of their own reactions and their own personalities, especially in relation to certain patients. For example, does he have the insight to recognize his tendency to be irritated at a querulous and demanding patient and thus to ignore his presuicidal communications? Every rescue operation is a dialogue: Someone cries for help and someone else must be willing to hear him and be capable of responding to him. Otherwise the victim may die because of the potential rescuer's unresponsiveness.

We must develop in ourselves a special attitude for suicide prevention. Each individual can be a lifesaver, a one-person committee to prevent suicide. Happily, elaborate pieces of mechanical equipment are not needed; "all" that is required are sharp eyes and ears, good intuition, a pinch of wisdom, an ability to act appropriately, and a deep resolve.

NOTES

1. N. L. Farberow and Edwin Shneidman, eds., *The Cry for Help* (New York: McGraw-Hill, 1961).

2. Robert Litman, "Emergency Response to Potential Suicide," *Journal of the Michigan Medical Society* 62 (1963): 68–72.

3. Norman L. Farberow, Edwin Shneidman, and Leonard Calista, *Suicide among General Medical and Surgical Hospital Patients with Malignant Neoplasms* (Washington, D.C.: Veterans' Administration, 1963).

4. Edwin Shneidman and Norman Farberow, *Evaluation and Treatment of Suicidal Risk among Schizophrenic Patients in Psychiatric Hospitals* (Washington, D. C.: Veterans' Administration, 1962).

5. Sherman Eisenthal, N. L. Farberow, and Edwin Shneidman, "Follow-up of Neuropsychiatric Hospital Patients on Suicide Observation Status," *Public Health Reports* 81 (November 1964): 977–90.

13

The Ethics of Suicide

Thomas S. Szasz

An editorial in the *Journal of the American Medical Association* (March 6, 1967) declared that "the contemporary physician sees suicide as a manifestation of emotional illness. Rarely does he view it in a context other than that of psychiatry." It was thus implied, the emphasis being the stronger for not being articulated, that to view suicide in this way is at once scientifically accurate and morally uplifting. I submit that it is neither; that, instead, this perspective on suicide is both erroneous and evil: erroneous because it treats an act as if it were a happening; and evil, because it serves to legitimize psychiatric force and fraud by justifying it as medical care and treatment.

Before going further, I should like to distinguish three fundamentally different concepts and categories that are combined and confused in most discussions of suicide. They are: (1) suicide proper, or so-called successful suicide; (2) attempted, threatened, or so-called unsuccessful suicide; and (3) the attribution by someone (typically a psychiatrist) to someone else (now called a "patient") of serious (that is, probably successful) suicidal intent. The first two concepts refer to acts by an actually or ostensibly

Reprinted from *The Antioch Review* 31 (Spring 1971):7–17, with the permission of the author. Copyright © 1971 by Thomas Szasz.

suicidal person; the third refers to the claim of an ostensibly normal person about someone else's suicide-proneness.

I believe that, generally speaking, the person who commits suicide intends to die; whereas the one who threatens suicide or makes an unsuccessful attempt at it intends to improve his life, not to terminate it. (The person who makes claims about someone else's suicidal intent does so usually in order to justify his efforts to control that person.)

Put differently, successful suicide is generally an expression of an individual's desire for greater autonomy—in particular, for self-control over his own death; whereas unsuccessful suicide is generally an expression of an individual's desire for more control over others—in particular, for compelling persons close to him to comply with his wishes. Although in some cases there may be legitimate doubt about which of these conditions obtains, in the majority of instances where people speak of "suicide" or "attempted suicide," the act falls clearly into one or the other group.

In short, I believe that successful and unsuccessful suicide constitute radically different acts or categories, and hence cannot be discussed together. Accordingly, I have limited the scope of this essay to suicide proper, with occasional references to attributions of suicidal intent. (The ascription of suicidal intent is, of course, a very different sort of thing from either successful or unsuccessful suicide. Since psychiatrists use it as if it designated a potentially or probably fatal "condition," it is sometimes necessary to consider this concept together with the phenomenon of suicide proper.)

I

It is difficult to find "responsible" medical or psychiatric authority today that does not regard suicide as a medical, and specifically as a mental health, problem.

For example, Ilza Veith, the noted medical historian, writing in *Modern Medicine* (August 11, 1969), asserts that "the act [of suicide] clearly represnts an illness. . . ."

Bernard R. Shochet, a psychiatrist at the University of Maryland, offers a precise description of the kind of illness it is. "Depression," he writes, "is a serious systemic disease, with both physiological and psychological concomitants, and suicide is a part of this syndrome." And he articulates the intervention he feels is implicit in this view: "If the patient's safety is in doubt, psychiatric hospitalization should be insisted on."[1]

Harvey M. Schein and Alan A. Stone, both psychiatrists at the Harvard Medical School, are even more explicit about the psychiatric coercion justified, in their judgment, by the threat of suicide. "Once the patient's suicidal thoughts are shared," they write,

> the therapist must take pains to make clear to the patient that he, the therapist, considers suicide to be a maladaptive action, irreversibly counter to the patient's sane interests and goals; that he, the therapist, will do *everything* he can do to prevent it; and that the potential for such an action arises from the patient's illness. It is equally essential that the therapist believe in the professional stance; if he does not he should not be treating the patient within the delicate human framework of psychotherapy.[2]

Schein and Stone do not explain why the patient's confiding in his therapist to the extent of communicating his suicidal thoughts to him should *ipso facto* deprive the patient from being the arbiter of his own best interests. The thrust of their argument is prescriptive rather than logical. They seek to justify depriving the patient of a basic human freedom—the freedom to grant or withhold consent for treatment: "The therapist must insist that patient and physician—*together*—communicate the suicidal potential to important figures in the environment, both professional and family. . . . Suicidal intent must not be part of therapeutic confidentiality." And further on they write: "Obviously this kind of patient must be hospitalized. . . . The therapist must be prepared to step in with hospitalization, with security measures, and with medication."

Schein and Stone thus suggest that the "suicidal" patient should have the right to choose his therapist; and that he should have the right to agree with his therapist and follow the latter's therapeutic recommendation (say, for hospitalization). At the same time, they insist that if "suicidal" patient and therapist disgree on therapy, then the patient should *not* have the right to disengage himself from the first therapist and choose a second—say, one who would consider suicidal intent a part of therapeutic confidentiality.

Many other psychiatric authorities could be cited to illustrate the current unanimity on this view of suicide.

Lawyers and jurists have eagerly accepted the psychiatric perspective on suicide, as they have on nearly everything else. An article in the *American Bar Association Journal* (September 1968) by R. E. Schulman, who is both a lawyer and a psychologist, is illustrative.

Schulman begins with the premise that "No one in contemporary Western society would suggest that people be allowed to commit suicide as they please without some attempt to intervene or prevent such suicides. Even if a person does not value his own life, Western society does value everyone's life."

But I should like to suggest, as others have suggested before me, precisely what Schulman claims no one would suggest. Furthermore, if Schulman chooses to believe that Western society—which includes the United States with its history of slavery, Germany with its history of National Socialism, and Russia with its history of Communism—really "values everyone's life," so be it. But to accept this assertion as true is to fly in the face of the most obvious and brutal facts of history.

II

When a person decides to take his life, and when a physician decides to frustrate him in this action, the question arises: Why should the physician do so?

Conventional psychiatric wisdom answers: Because the suicidal person (now called "patient" for proper emphasis) suffers from a mental illness whose symptom is his desire to kill himself; it is the physician's duty to diagnose and treat his illness: *ergo,* he must prevent the "patient" from killing himself and, at the same time, must "treat" the underlying "disease" that "causes" the "patient" to wish doing away with himself. This looks like an ordinary medical diagnosis and intervention. But it is not. What is missing? Everything. The hypothetical, suicidal "patient" is not ill; he has no demonstrable bodily disorder (or if he does, it does not "cause" his suicide); he does not assume the sick role: he does not seek medical help. In short, the physician uses the rhetoric of illness and treatment to justify his forcible intervention in the life of a fellow human being—often in the face of explicit opposition from his so-called "patient."

I do not doubt that attempted or successful suicide may be exceedingly *disturbing* for persons related to, acquainted with, or caring for the ostensible "patient." But I reject the conclusion that the suicidal person is, *ipso facto,* disturbed, that being disturbed equals being *mentally ill,* and that being mentally ill *justifies* psychiatric hospitalization or treatment. I have developed my reasons for this elsewhere, and need not repeat them here.[3] For the sake of emphasis, however, let me state that I consider counseling, persuasion, psychotherapy, or any other *voluntary measure*, especially for persons troubled by their own suicidal inclinations and seeking such help, unobjectionable, and indeed generally desirable, interventions. However, physicians and psychiatrists are usually not satisfied with limiting their help to such measures—and with good reason: from such assistance the individual may gain not only the desire to live, but also the strength to die.

But we still have not answered the question: Why should a physician frustrate an individual from killing himself? As we saw, some psychiatrists answer: Because the physician values the patient's life, at least when the patient is suicidal, more highly than does the patient himself. Let us examine this claim. Why should the physician, often a complete stranger to the suicidal patient, value the patient's life more highly than does the patient himself? He does not do so in medical practice. Why then should he do so in psychiatric practice, which he himself insists is a form of medical practice? Let us assume that a physician is confronted with an individual suffering from diabetes or heart failure who fails to take the drugs prescribed for his illness. We know that this often happens, and that when it does the patient may become disabled and die prematurely. Yet it would be absurd for a physician to consider, much less attempt, taking over the conduct of such a patient's life, confining him in a hospital against his will in order to treat his disease. Indeed, any attempt to do so would bring the physician into conflict with both the civil and the criminal law. For, significantly, the law recognizes the medical patient's autonomy despite the fact that, unlike the suicidal individual, he suffers from a real disease; and despite the fact that, unlike the nonexistent disease of the suicidal individual, his illness is often easily controlled by simple and safe therapeutic procedures.

Nevertheless, the threat of alleged or real suicide, or so-called dangerousness to oneself, is everywhere considered a proper ground and justification for involuntary mental hospitalization and treatment. Why should this be so?

Let me suggest what I believe is likely to be the most important reason for the profound anti-suicidal bias of the medical profession. Physicians are committed to saving lives. How, then, should they react to people who are committed to throwing away their lives? It is natural for people to dislike, indeed to hate, those who challenge their basic values. The physician thus reacts, perhaps "unconsciously" (in the sense that he does not articulate the problem in these terms), to the suicidal patient as if the patient had affronted, insulted, or attacked him: The physician strives valiantly, often at the cost of his own well-being, to save lives; and here comes a person who not only does not let the physician save him, but, *horribile dictu,* makes the physician an unwilling witness to that person's deliberate self-destruction. This is more than most physicians can take. Feeling assaulted in the very center of their spiritual identity, some take to flight, while others fight back.

Some nonpsychiatric physicians will thus have nothing to do with suicidal patients. This explains why many people who end up killing themselves have a record of having consulted a physician, often on the very day of their suicide. I surmise that these persons go in search of help, only to discover that the physician wants nothing to do with them. And, in a sense, it is right that it should be so. I do not blame the doctors. Nor do I advocate teaching them suicide prevention—whatever that might be. I contend that because physicians have a relatively blind faith in their life-saving ideology—which, moreover, they often need to carry them through their daily work—they are the wrong people for listening and talking to individuals, intelligently and calmly, about suicide. So much for those physicians who, in the face of the existential attack which they feel the suicidal patient launches on them, run for *their* lives. Let us now look at those who stand and fight back.

Some physicians (and other mental health professionals) declare themselves not only ready and willing to help suicidal patients who seek assistance, but all persons who are, or are alleged to be, suicidal. Since they, too, seem to perceive suicide as a threat, not just to the suicidal person's physical survival but to their own value system, they strike back and strike back hard. This explains why psychiatrists and suicidologists resort, apparently with a perfectly clear conscience, to the vilest methods: they must believe that their lofty ends justify the basest means. Hence the prevalent use of force and fraud in suicide prevention. The consequence of this kind of interaction between physician and "patient" is a struggle for power. The patient is at least honest about what he wants: to gain control over his life *and* death—by being the agent of his own demise. But the (suicide-preventing) psychiatrist is completely dishonest about what he wants: he claims that he only wants to help his patient, while actually he wants to gain control over the patient's life in order to save himself from having to confront his doubts about the value of his own life. Suicide is medical heresy. Commitment and electroshock are the appropriate psychiatric-inquisitorial remedies for it.

III

In the West, opposition to suicide, like opposition to contraception and abortion, rests on religious grounds. According to both the Jewish and Christian religions, God created man, and man can use himself only in the ways permitted by God. Preventing conception, aborting a pregnancy, or killing oneself are, in this imagery, all sins: each is a violation of the laws laid down by God, or by theological authorities claiming to speak in His name.

But modern man is a revolutionary. Like all revolutionaries, he likes to take away from those who have and to give to those who have not, especially himself. He has thus taken Man from God and given him to the State (with which he often identifies more than he knows). This is why the State gives and takes away so many of our rights, and why we consider this arrangement so "natural."

But this arrangement leaves suicide in a peculiar moral and philo-sophical limbo. For if a man's life belongs to the State (as it formerly belonged to God), then surely suicide is the taking of a life that belongs not to the taker but to everyone else.

The dilemma of this simplistic transfer of body-ownership from God to State derives from the fundamental difference between a religious and secular world view, especially when the former entails a vivid conception of a life after death, whereas the latter does not (or even emphatically repudiates it). More particularly, the dilemma derives from the problem of how to punish successful suicide. Traditionally, the Roman Catholic Church punished it by depriving the suicide of burial in consecrated ground. As far as I know, this practice is now so rare in the United States as to be practically nonexistent. Suicides are given a Catholic burial, as they are routinely considered having taken their lives while insane.

The modern State, with psychiatry as its secular-religious ally, has no comparable sanction to offer. Could this be one of the reasons why it punishes so severely—so very much more severely than did the Church —the *unsuccessful* suicide? For I consider the psychiatric stigmatization of people as "suicidal risks" and their incarceration in psychiatric institu-tions a form of punishment, and a very severe one at that. Indeed, al-though I cannot support this claim with statistics, I believe that accepted psychiatric methods of suicide prevention often aggravate rather than ameliorate the suicidal person's problems. As one reads of the tragic en-counters with psychiatry of people like James Forrestal, Marilyn Monroe, or Ernest Hemingway, one gains the impression that they felt demeaned and deeply hurt by the psychiatric indignities inflicted on them, and that, as a result of these experiences, they were even more desperately driven to suicide. In short, I am suggesting that coerced psychiatric interventions may increase, rather than diminish, the suicidal person's desire for self-destruction.

But there is another aspect of the moral and philosophical dimensions of suicide that must be mentioned here. I refer to the growing influence of the resurgent idea of self-determination, especially the conviction that men have certain inalienable rights. Some men have thus come to believe (or perhaps only to believe that they believe) that they have a right to life, liberty, and property. This makes for some interesting complications for the modern legal and psychiatric stand on suicide.

This individualistic position on suicide might be put thus: A man's life belongs to himself. Hence, he has a right to take his own life, that is, to commit suicide. To be sure, this view recognizes that a man may also have a moral responsibility to his family and others, and that, by killing himself, he reneges on these reponsibilities. But these are moral wrongs that society, in its corporate capacity as the State, cannot properly punish. Hence the State must eschew attempts to regulate such behavior by means of formal sanctions, such as criminal or mental hygiene laws.

The analogy between life and other types of property lends further support to this line of argument. Having a right to property means that a person can dispose of it even if in so doing he injures himself and his family. A man may give away, or gamble away, his money. But significantly, he cannot—our linguistic conventions do not allow it—be said to *steal from himself*. The concept of theft requires at least two parties: one who steals and another from whom something is stolen. There is no such thing as "self-theft." The term "suicide" blurs this very distinction. The etymology of this term implies that suicide is a type of homicide, one in which criminal and victim are one and the same person. Indeed, when a person wants to condemn suicide he calls it "self-murder." Schulman, for example, writes: "Surely, self-murder falls within the province of the law."

History does repeat itself. Until recently, psychiatrists castigated as sick and persecuted those who engaged in self-abuse (that is, masturbation); now they castigate as sick and persecute those who engage in self-murder (that is, suicide).

The suicidologist has a literally schizophrenic view of the suicidal person: He sees him as two persons in one, each at war with the other. One half of the patient wants to die; the other half wants to live. The former, says the suicidologist, is wrong; the latter is right. And he proceeds to protect the latter by restraining the former. However, since these two people are, like Siamese twins, one, he can restrain the suicidal half only by restraining the whole person.

The absurdity of this medical-psychiatric position on suicide does not end here. It ends in extolling mental health and physical survival over every other value, particularly individual liberty.

In regarding the desire to live as a legitimate human aspiration, but not the desire to die, the suicidologist stands Patrick Henry's famous exclamation, "Give me liberty, or give me death!" on its head. In effect, he says: "*Give him* commitment, *give him* electroshock, *give him* lobotomy, *give him* life-long slavery, but *do not let him choose* death!" By so radically invalidating another person's (not his own!) wish to die, the suicide-preventer redefines the aspiration of the Other as not an aspiration at all: The wish to die thus becomes something an irrational, mentally diseased being displays, or something that happens to a lower form of life. The result is a far-reaching infantilization and dehumanization of the suicidal person.

For example, Phillip Solomon writes in the *Journal of the American Medical Association* (January 30, 1967), that "We [physicians] must protect the patient from his own [suicidal] wishes." While to Edwin Shneidman, "Suicide prevention is like fire prevention."[4] Solomon thus reduces the would-be suicide to the level of an unruly child, while Shneidman reduces him to the level of a tree! In short, the suicidologist uses his professional stance to illegitimize and punish the wish to die.

There is, of course, nothing new about any of this. Do-gooders have always opposed autonomy or self-determination. In "Amok," written in 1931, Stefan Zweig put these words into the mouth of his protagonist: "Ah, yes, 'It's one's duty to help.' That's your famous maxim, isn't it? . . . Thank you for your good intentions, but I'd rather be left to myself. . . . So I won't trouble you to call, if you don't mind. Among the 'rights of man' there is a right which no one can take away, the right to croak when and where and how one pleases, without a 'helping hand.' "

But this is not the way the scientific psychiatrist and suicidologist sees the problem. He might agree (I suppose) that, in the abstract, man has the right Zweig claimed for him. But, in practice, suicide (so he says) is the result of insanity, madness, mental illness. Furthermore, it makes no sense to say that one has a right to be mentally ill, especially if the illness is one that, like typhoid fever, threatens the health of other people as well. In short, the suicidologist's job is to try to convince people that wanting to die is a disease.

This is how Ari Kiev, director of the Cornell Program in Social Psychiatry and its suicide-prevention clinic, does it: "We say [to the patient], look, you have a disease, just like the Hong Kong flu. Maybe you've got the Hong Kong depression. First, you've got to realize you are emotionally ill. . . . Most of the patients have never admitted to themselves that they are sick . . . ." (*New York Times*, February 9, 1969).

This pseudomedical perspective is then used to justify psychiatric deception and coercion of the crudest sort.

Here is how, according to the *Wall Street Journal* (March 6, 1969), the Los Angeles Suicide Prevention Center operates. A man calls and says he is about to shoot himself. The worker asks for his address. The man refuses to give it.

"If I pull it [the trigger] now I'll be dead," he [the caller] said in a muffled voice. "And that's what I want." Silently but urgently, Mrs. Whitbook [the worker] has signalled a co-worker to begin tracing the call. And now she worked to keep the man talking. . . . An agonizing 40 minutes passed. Then she heard the voice of a policeman come on the phone to say the man was safe.

But surely, if this man was able to call the Suicide Prevention Center, he could have, had he wanted, called for a policeman himself. But he did not. He was thus deceived by the Center in the "service" he got.

I understand that this kind of deception is a standard practice in suicide prevention centers, though it is often denied that it is. A report (*Medical World News*, July 28, 1967) about the Nassau County Suicide Prevention Service corroborates the impression that when the would-be suicide does not cooperate with the suicide-prevention authorities, he is confined involuntarily. "When a caller is obviously suicidal," we are told, "a Meadowbrook ambulance is sent out immediately to pick him up."

One more example of the sort of thing that goes on in the name of suicide prevention should suffice. It is a routine story from a Syracuse newspaper (Syracuse *Post Standard*, September 29, 1969). The gist of it is all in one sentence: "A 28-year-old Minoa [a Syracuse suburb] man was arrested last night on a charge of violation of the Mental Hygiene Law, after police authorities said they spent two hours looking for him in the Minoa woods." But this man has harmed no one; his only "offense" was that someone claimed he might harm himself. Why, then, should the police look for, much less arrest, him? Why not wait until he returns? Or why not look, offer help, but avoid arrest and coerced psychiatry?

These are rhetorical questions. For our answers to them depend on and reflect our concepts of what it means to be a human being.

IV

I submit, then, that the crucial contradiction about suicide viewed as an illness whose treatment is a medical responsibility is that suicide is an action but is treated as if it were a happening. As I showed elsewhere, this contradiction lies at the heart of all so-called mental illnesses or psychiatric problems.[5] However, it poses a particularly acute dilemma for suicide, because suicide is the only fatal "mental illness."

Before concluding, I should like to restate briefly my views on the differences between diseases and desires, and show that by persisting in treating desires as diseases, we only end up treating man as a slave.

Let us take, as our paradigm case of illness, a skier who takes a bad spill and fractures an ankle. This fracture is something that has happened to him. He has not intended it to happen. (To be sure, he may have intended it; but that is another case.) Once it has happened, he will seek medical help and will cooperate with medical efforts to mend his broken bones. In short, the person and his fractured ankle are, as it were, two separate entities, the former acting on the latter.

Let us now consider the case of the suicidal person. Such a person may also look upon his own suicidal inclination as an undesired, almost alien, impulse and seek help to combat it. If so, the ensuing arrangement between him and his psychiatrist is readily assimilated to the standard medical model of treatment: the patient actively seeks and cooperates with professional efforts to remedy his "condition."

But as we have seen this is not the only way, nor perhaps the most important way, that the game of suicide prevention is played. It is accepted medical and psychiatric practice to treat persons for their suicidal desires against their will. And what exactly does this mean? Something quite different from that to which it is often analogized, namely the involuntary (or nonvoluntary) treatment of a bodily illiness. For a fractured ankle can be set whether or not a patient consents to its being set. That is because setting a fracture is a *mechanical act on the body.* But a threatened suicide cannot be prevented whether or not the "patient" consents to its being prevented. That is because, suicide being the result of human desire and action, suicide prevention is a *political act on the person.* In other words, since suicide is an exercise and expression of human freedom, it can be prevented only by curtailing human freedom. This is why deprivation of liberty becomes, in institutional psychiatry, a form of treatment.

In the final analysis, the would-be suicide is like the would-be emigrant: both want to leave where they are and move elsewhere. The suicide wants to leave life and embrace death. The emigrant wants to leave his homeland and settle in another country.

Let us take this analogy seriously. It is much more faithful to the facts than is the analogy between suicide and illness. A crucial characteristic that distinguishes open from closed societies is that people are free to leave the former but not the latter. The medical profession's stance toward suicide is thus like the Communists' toward emigration: the doctors insist that the would-be suicide survive, just as the Russians insist that the would-be emigrant stay home.

Whether those who so curtail other people's liberties act with complete sincerity, or with utter cynicism, hardly matters. What matters is what happens: the abridgement of individual liberty, justified, in the case of suicide prevention, by psychiatric rhetoric; and, in the case of emigration prevention, by political rhetoric.

In language and logic we are the prisoners of our premises, just as in politics and law we are the prisoners of our rulers. Hence we had better pick them well. For if suicide is an illness because it terminates in death, and if the prevention of death by any means necessary is the physician's therapeutic mandate, then the proper remedy for suicide is indeed liberticide.

NOTES

1. Bernard Shochet, "Recognizing the Suicidal Patient," *Modern Medicine* 38 (May 1970):114–23.

2. Harvey M. Schein and Alan A. Stone, "Psychotherapy Designed to Detect and Treat Suicidal Potential," *American Journal of Psychiatry* 125 (March 1969): 1247–51 (emphasis added).

3. Thomas S. Szasz, *Law, Liberty and Psychiatry* (New York: Macmillan, 1963); and *Ideology and Insanity* (Garden City, N.Y.: Doubleday, 1970).

4. Edwin Shneidman, "Preventing Suicide," *Bulletin of Suicidology* (July 1968): 19–25 [see chapter 12 in this volume].

5. Thomas S. Szasz, *The Myth of Mental Illness* (New York: Harper and Row, 1961).

14

Theistic and Nontheistic Arguments

Milton A. Gonsalves

Suicide is here taken in the strict sense as *the direct killing of oneself on one's own authority.*

Direct killing is an act of killing that is directly voluntary; that is, death is intended either as an end or as a means to an end. Either the action is capable of only one effect and that effect is death, or the action is capable of several effects, including death, and among these death is the effect intended, either for its own sake or as a means to something else.

Indirect killing is an act of killing that is indirectly voluntary; death is not intended, either as an end or as a means to an end, but is only permitted as an unavoidable consequence. The action is capable of at least two effects, one of which is death, and the agent intends, not death, but the other effect. To avoid misunderstanding it is better not to speak of the indirect killing of oneself as killing at all, but as the deliberate exposure of one's life to serious danger. Such exposure is not what is meant by suicide.

From Milton A. Gonsalves, "Suicide," in *Fagothey's Right and Reason: Ethics in Theory and Practice* (Columbus: Merrill Publishing Co., 1989), pp. 246–48. Reprinted by permission of the publisher.

The killing is not suicide unless it is done *on one's own authority.* Two others might be thought of as having authority in the matter: God and the state. God, having a supreme dominion over human life, could order a woman to kill herself, but to know God's will in such a case, a special revelation would be needed, for which there is no provision in philosophical ethics. The state, supposing that it has the right of capital punishment, might appoint a man condemned to death to be his own executioner. Whatever be the morality of such an uncommon and questionable practice, it is not suicide according to the accepted definition.

Suicide can be committed positively, by the performance of some death-dealing act against oneself; or negatively, by omitting to use the ordinary means of preserving one's life. It is suicide to starve oneself to death, to refuse to avoid an oncoming train, to neglect to use the ordinary remedies against an otherwise fatal disease.

Among the arguments proposed in favor of the moral permissibility of suicide are the following:

1. It is understood that no one should commit suicide for whom life holds out some hope or promise, and that people suffering from temporary despondency should be prevented from harming themselves, but there are always some for whom life has become an intolerable and irremediable burden. They are useless to society and to themselves. It is better for all concerned that they retire from the scene of life through the ever open door.

2. It is an act of supreme personal self-determination to summon death when life's value has been spent. A person is expected to manage his or her life intelligently and not to be merely passive in the face of inexorable nature. When reason shows that life has no more to offer, it is folly to drag out life to its last bitter breath. The person preserves dignity and self-mastery by ending his or her life at the moment when all its worth and meaning are exhausted.

3. A person is allowed to choose a lesser evil to avoid a greater. Since there are worse evils than death, why cannot death be chosen as the lesser evil? There is nothing unnatural about it. If it is not wrong to interfere with nature to prolong life, as medical science does, why should it be wrong to interfere with nature to shorten life? In both cases it is done for the benefit of the person concerned and by his or her own consent.

4. Even admitting that God has given us our life, yet it is truly a gift. A gift belongs to the receiver, who may now do whatever he or she

wills with it. No gift is expected to be retained indefinitely at the expense and to the harm of the receiver. When its possession becomes more injurious than its surrender, it should be in accordance with the will of a good God and a wise use of his gift to relinquish it.

5. To suppose that suicide in any way defrauds God of his supreme right is to have a very naive idea of God. No creature could possibly defraud God of anything. In giving us the gift of life, God knew how we would use it and expected us to use our intelligence and freedom in managing it. He allows us to destroy animals and plants, other life, for our purposes. Why should our own life be withdrawn from our control?

6. In the case of self-defense we have the right to destroy other human lives for our own safety. The state claims the same right in war and capital punishment. It seems, then, that God can and sometimes does give us direct ownership over human life. Why must it be only over others' lives? The reasons for suicide are often stronger than for self-defense, either personal or national. Why not kill ourselves when we have become our own greatest enemy?

These rather persuasive arguments are countered by opposing arguments:

1. Suicide is often regarded as an act of cowardice and a refusal to face life courageously. We take the easy way out when we thrust the burdens we cannot bear onto the shoulders of our dependents. But not all are in this case; rather, they themselves are a burden on others. Yet they must not forget the worth of their own person. Who can be called useless? Suffering has no earthly value and might be called the worst of earthly disvalues, but its moral and spiritual value can be tremendous. Courage and patience cannot be discounted in any moral appraisal of human life.

2. It is a natural prompting of well-ordered self-love to keep one's person in being against all destructive forces. There are times when one must face death without flinching, but there is something inordinate in willfully acting as that destructive force oneself. Everything naturally seeks its own being and tends to keep itself in being as long as possible. Intelligence is meant to promote, not counteract, that natural urge.

3. The lesser of two physical evils may be chosen when there is no moral evil involved, but moral evil may never be chosen to avoid a physical evil. Medical science is an intelligent use and development of the remedies nature provides to preserve life. To use them to destroy life is not wise management but a wrecking of what has been entrusted to our care. I would be free to wreck myself if I were responsible only to myself, but

this is not so if there is a God to whom I am ultimately responsible.

4. Life is a gift from God, but some gifts are given outright and others have strings attached. All God's gifts are restricted, not because of any lack in his generosity, but because he has to make us responsible for their use when he entrusts them to our freedom. Freedom itself is perhaps his greatest gift, but we are not allowed, though we are able, to misuse it. Life has been given, and its allotted span goes with the gift. It is not ours to decide when we have had enough of it and to tell God that we are quitting.

5. We can never actually defraud God, but we are not allowed even to *try* or to be willing to do what would defraud God were he not infinitely beyond all possible harm. God allows us to destroy animals and plants because they are not persons and are provided for our use and consumption. Human life is not on the same level as other life; personhood makes the difference.

6. In self-defense the defender kills the attacker not on his or her own authority but on God's authority implicit in the defender's own natural right to life. The defender has no ownership over the attacker's life but only repels force by force, a situation the attacker brought on by the crime. The state also acts on authority given to it by God as a natural society, authority not to be used in any way the state pleases but only in defense against the nation's internal and external destroyers. The suicide is both attacker and attacked, and there is no defense. Crime and punishment are here simultaneous and extreme. The suicide is simultaneously executioner and murderer.

It can be readily seen that from a nontheistic viewpoint there is no argument against suicide. A person who acknowledges no being higher than himself or herself assumes supreme dominion over his or her life and can do away with it at pleasure. The fact that a theistic philosophy sees life as a gift from God does not of itself make suicide wrong, for an outright gift may be used or abandoned in any way the recipient wishes. The case against suicide, then, requires proof that God's gift of life to us is not an outright but a restricted gift, that he has not given us full ownership and control over our person with the right to consume and destroy it at our discretion, but he has given us only the use of ourselves, the right of stewardship and management, for which he will demand an account. Since philosophy cannot ask God what he willed to do, its only recourse is to show that God not only did not but *could not* give us full ownership over ourselves as persons.

The reason that God must reserve to himself full mastership over human life is the peculiar nature of a rational and free being, such as the human being is. We can attain the end for which we have been created only by freely choosing to do morally good acts. These acts take time, and the length of each person's life is the opportunity allotted for doing them. It is for God and not for us to say when we have done enough well enough to deserve the end. The suicide equivalently tells God that He will have to take the deeds performed and virtues developed so far, and that He will simply get no more. The creature thus tries to dictate what God will have to be satisfied with, in contradiction to what God in creating has a right to demand from His creature. God cannot give such authority to a creature without making the creature supreme over Him. The suicide, by making further works of his or her own impossible, invades God's exclusive right, is a rebel against the creator, and commits moral wrong.

15

The Morality and Rationality of Suicide

Richard B. Brandt

From the point of view of contemporary philosophy, suicide raises the following distinct questions: whether a person who commits suicide (assuming that there is suicide if and only if there is intentional termination of one's own life) is morally blameworthy, reprehensible, sinful in all circumstances; whether suicide is objectively right or wrong, and in what circumstances it is right or wrong, from a moral point of view; and whether, or in which circumstances, suicide is the best or the rational thing to do from the point of view of the agent's personal welfare.

THE MORAL BLAMEWORTHINESS OF SUICIDE

In former times the question of whether suicide is sinful was of great interest because the answer to it was considered relevant to how the agent would spend eternity. At present the practical issue is not as great, al-

Originally published in the *Handbook for the Study of Suicide*, edited by Seymour Perlin, pp. 61–76. Copyright © 1975 by Oxford University Press, Inc. Reprinted by permission.

though a normal funeral service may be denied a person judged to have committed suicide sinfully. The chief practical issue now seems to be that persons may disapprove of a decedent for having committed suicide, and his friends or relatives may wish to defend his memory against moral charges.

The question of whether an act of suicide was sinful or morally blameworthy is not apt to arise unless it is already believed that the agent morally ought not to have done it: for instance, if he really had very poor reason for doing so, and his act foreseeably had catastrophic consequences for his wife and children. But, even if a given suicide is morally wrong, it does not follow that it is morally reprehensible. For, while asserting that a given act of suicide was wrong, we may still think that the act was hardly morally blameworthy or sinful if, say, the agent was in a state of great emotional turmoil at the time. We might then say that, although what he did was wrong, his action is *excusable,* just as in the criminal law it may be decided that, although a person broke the law, he should not be punished because he was *not responsible,* that is, was temporarily insane, did what he did inadvertently, and so on.

The foregoing remarks assume that to be morally blameworthy (or sinful) on account of an act is one thing, and for the act to be wrong is another. But, if we say this, what after all does it *mean* to say that a person is morally blameworthy on account of an action? We cannot say there is agreement among philosophers on this matter, but I suggest the following account as being safe from serious objection: "X is morally blameworthy on account of an action A" may be taken to mean "X did A, and X would not have done A had not his character been in some respect below standard; and in view of this it is fitting or justified for X to have some disapproving attitudes including remorse toward himself, and for some other persons Y to have some disapproving attitudes toward X and to express them in behavior." Traditional thought would include God as one of the "other persons" who might have and express disapproving attitudes.

In case the foregoing definition does not seem obviously correct, it is worthwhile pointing out that it is usually thought that an agent is not blameworthy or sinful for an action unless it is a *reflection on him;* the definition brings this fact out and makes clear why.

If someone charges that a suicide was sinful, we may now properly ask, "What defect of character did it show?" Some writers have claimed that suicide is blameworthy because it is *cowardly,* and since being cowardly is generally conceded to be a defect of character, if an act of suicide is admitted to be both objectively wrong and also cowardly, the claim to blameworthiness might be warranted in terms of the above definition. Of course, many people would hesitate to call taking one's own life a cowardly act, and there will certainly be controversy about which acts are cowardly and which are not. But at least we can see part of what has to be done to make a charge of blameworthiness valid.

The most interesting question is the general one: which types of suicide in general are ones that, even if objectively wrong (in a sense to be explained below), are not sinful or blameworthy? Or, in other words, when is a suicide *morally excused* even if it is objectively wrong? We can at least identify some types that are morally excusable.

1. Suppose I *think* I am morally bound to commit suicide because I have a terminal illness and continued medical care will ruin my family financially. Suppose, however, that I am mistaken in this belief, and that suicide in such circumstances is not right. But surely I am not morally blameworthy; for I may be doing, out of a sense of duty to my family, what I would personally prefer not to do and is hard for me to do. What defect of character might my action show? Suicide from a genuine sense of duty is not blameworthy, even when the moral conviction in question is mistaken.

2. Suppose that I commit suicide when I am temporarily of unsound mind, either in the sense of the M'Naghten rule that I do not know that what I am doing is wrong, or of the Durham rule that, owing to a mental defect, I am substantially unable to do what is right. Surely, any suicide in an unsound state of mind is morally excused.

3. Suppose I commit suicide when I could not be said to be temporarily of unsound mind, but simply because I am not myself. For instance, I may be in an extremely depressed mood. Now a person may be in a very depressed mood, and commit suicide on account of being in that mood, when there is nothing the matter with his character—or, in other words, his character is not in any relevant way below standard. What are other examples of being "not myself," of emotional states that might be responsible for a person's committing suicide, and that might render the suicide excusable even if wrong? Being frightened; being distraught; being in almost any highly emotional frame of mind (anger, frustration, disappointment in love); perhaps just being terribly fatigued.

So there are at least three types of suicide which can be morally excused even if they are objectively wrong. The main point is this: Mr. X may commit suicide and it may be conceded that he ought not to have done so, but it is another step to show that he is sinful, or morally blameworthy, for having done so. To make out that further point, it must be shown that his act is attributable to some substandard trait of character. So, Mrs. X after the suicide can concede that her husband ought not to have done what he did, but she can also point out that it is no reflection on his character. The distinction, unfortunately, is often overlooked. St. Thomas Aquinas, who recognizes the distinction in other places, seems blind to it in his discussion of suicide.

THE MORAL REASONS FOR AND AGAINST SUICIDE

Persons who say suicide is morally wrong must be asked which of two positions they are affirming: Are they saying that *every* act of suicide is wrong, *everything considered;* or are they merely saying that there is always *some* moral obligation—doubtless of serious weight—not to commit suicide, so that very often suicide is wrong, although it is possible that there are *countervailing considerations* which in particular situations make it right or even a moral duty? It is quite evident that the first position is absurd; only the second has a chance of being defensible.

In order to make clear what is wrong with the first view, we may begin with an example. Suppose an army pilot's single-seater plane goes out of control over a heavily populated area; he has the choice of staying in the plane and bringing it down where it will do little damage but at the cost of certain death for himself, and of bailing out and letting the plane fall where it will, very possibly killing a good many civilians. Suppose he chooses to do the former, and so, by our definition, commits suicide. Does anyone want to say that his action is morally wrong? Even Immanuel Kant, who opposed suicide in all circumstances, apparently would not wish to say that it is; he would, in fact, judge that this act is not one of suicide, for he says, "It is no suicide to risk one's life against one's enemies, and even to sacrifice it, in order to preserve one's duties towards oneself."[1] St. Thomas Aquinas, in his discussion of suicide, may seem to take the position that such an act would be wrong, for he says, "It is altogether unlawful to kill oneself," admitting as an exception only the case of being under special command of God. But I believe St. Thomas would, in fact, have concluded that the act is right because the basic intention of the pilot was to save the lives of civilians, and whether an act is right or wrong is a matter of basic intention.[2]

In general, we have to admit that there are things with some moral obligation to avoid which, on account of other morally relevant considerations, it is sometimes right or even morally obligatory to do. There may be some obligation to tell the truth on every occasion, but surely in many cases the consequences of telling the truth would be so dire that one is obligated to lie. The same goes for promises. There is some moral obligation to do what one has promised (with a few exceptions); but, if one can keep a trivial promise only at serious cost to another person (i.e., keep an appointment only by failing to give aid to someone injured in an accident), it is surely obligatory to break the promise.

The most that the moral critic of suicide could hold, then, is that there is *some* moral obligation not to do what one knows will cause one's death; but he surely cannot deny that circumstances exist in which there are obligations to do things which, in fact, will result in one's death. If so, then in principle it would be possible to argue, for instance, that in order to meet my obligation to my family, it might be right for me to take my own life as the only way to avoid catastrophic hospital expenses in a terminal illness. Possibly the main point that critics of suicide on moral grounds would wish to make it that it is never right to take one's own life *for reasons of one's own personal welfare,* of any kind whatsoever. Some of the arguments used to support the immorality of suicide, however, are so framed that if they were supportable at all, they would prove that suicide is *never* moral.

One well-known type of argument against suicide may be classified as *theological.* St. Augustine and others urged that the Sixth Commandment ("Thou shalt not kill") prohibits suicide, and that we are bound to obey a divine commandment. To this reasoning one might first reply that it is arbitrary exegesis of the Sixth Commandment to assert that it was intended to prohibit suicide. The second reply is that if there is not some consideration which shows on the merits of the case that suicide is morally wrong, God has no business prohibiting it. It is true that some will object to this point, and I must refer them elsewhere for my detailed comments on the divine-will theory of morality.[3]

Another theological argument with wide support was accepted by John Locke, who wrote: ". . . Men being all the workmanship of one omnipotent and infinitely wise Maker; all the servants of one sovereign Master, sent into the world by His order and about His business; they are His property, whose workmanship they are made to last during His, not one another's pleasure. . . . Every one . . . is bound to preserve himself, and not to quit his station wilfully. . . ."⁴ And Kant: "We have been placed in this world under certain conditions and for specific purposes. But a suicide opposes the purpose of his Creator; he arrives in the other world as one who has deserted his post; he must be looked upon as a rebel against God. So long as we remember the truth that it is God's intention to preserve life, we are bound to regulate our activities in conformity with it. This duty is upon us until the time comes when God expressly commands us to leave this life. Human beings are sentinels on earth and may not leave their posts until relieved by another beneficent hand."⁵ Unfortunately, however, even if we grant that it is the duty of human beings to do what God commands or intends them to do, more argument is required to show that God does *not* permit human beings to quit this life when their own personal welfare would be maximized by so doing. How does one draw the requisite inference about the intentions of God? The difficulties and contradictions in arguments to reach such a conclusion are discussed at length and perspicaciously by David Hume in his essay "On Suicide," and in view of the unlikelihood that readers will need to be persuaded about these, I shall merely refer those interested to that essay.⁶

A second group of arguments may be classed as arguments *from natural law*. St. Thomas says: "It is altogether unlawful to kill oneself, for three reasons. First, because everything naturally loves itself, the result being that everything naturally keeps itself in being, and resists corruptions as far as it can. Wherefore suicide is contrary to the inclination of nature, and to charity whereby every man should love himself. Hence suicide is always a mortal sin, as being contrary to the natural law and to charity."⁷ Here St. Thomas ignores two obvious points. First, it is not obvious why a human being is morally bound to do what he or she has some inclination to do. (St. Thomas did not criticize chastity.) Second, while it is true that most human beings do feel a strong urge to live, the human being who commits suicide obviously feels a stonger inclination to do something else. It is as natural for a human being to dislike, and to take steps to avoid, say, great pain, as it is to cling to life.

A somewhat similar argument by Immanuel Kant may seem better. In a famous passage Kant writes that the maxim of a person who commits suicide is "From self-love I make it my principle to shorten my life if its continuance threatens more evil than it promises pleasure. The only further question to ask is whether this principle of self-love can become a universal law of nature. It is then seen at once that a system of nature by whose law the very same feeling whose function is to stimulate the furtherance of life should actually destroy life would contradict itself and consequently would not subsist as a system of nature. Hence this maxim cannot possibly hold as a universal law of nature and is therefore entirely opposed to the supreme principle of all duty."⁸ What Kant finds contradictory is that the motive of self-love (interest in one's own long-range welfare) should sometimes lead one to struggle to preserve one's life, but at other times to end it. But where is the contradiction? One's circumstances change, and, if the argument of the following section in this chapter is correct, one sometimes maximizes one's own long-range welfare by trying to stay alive, but at other times by bringing about one's demise.

A third group of arguments, a form of which goes back at least to Aristotle, has a more modern and convincing ring. These are arguments to show that, in one way or another, a suicide necessarily does harm to other persons, or to society at large. Aristotle says that the suicide treats the *state* unjustly.⁹ Partly following Aristotle, St. Thomas says: "Every man is part of the communty, and so, as such, he belongs to the community. Hence by killing himself he injures the community."¹⁰ Blackstone held that a suicide is an offense against the king "who hath an interest in the preservation of all his subjects," perhaps following Judge Brown in 1563, who argued that suicide cost the king a subject—"he being the head has lost one of his mystical members."¹¹ The premise of such arguments is, as Hume pointed out, obviously mistaken in many instances. It is true that Freud would perhaps have injured society had he, instead of finishing his last book, committed suicide to escape the pain of throat cancer. But surely there have been many suicides whose demise was not a noticeable loss to society; an honest man could only say that in some instances society was better off without them.

It need not be denied that suicide is often injurious to other persons, especially the family of a suicide. Clearly it sometimes is. But, we should notice what this fact establishes. Suppose we admit, as generally would be done, that there is some obligation not to perform any action which will probably or certainly be injurious to other people, the strength of the obligation being dependent on various factors, notably the seriousness of the expected injury. Then there is *some* obligation not to commit suicide, when that act would probably or certainly be injurious to other people. But, as we have already seen, many cases of *some* obligation to do something nevertheless are *not* cases of a duty to do that thing, *everything considered.* So it could sometimes be morally justified to commit suicide, even if the act will harm someone. Must a man with a terminal illness undergo excruciating pain because his death will cause his wife sorrow—when she will be caused sorrow a month later anyway, when he is dead of natural causes? Moreover, to repeat, the fact that an individual has some obligation not to commit suicide when that act will probably injure other persons does not imply that, everything considered, it is wrong for him to do it, namely, that in all circumstances suicide *as such* is something there is some obligation to avoid.

Is there any sound argument, convincing to the modern mind, to establish that there is (or is not) *some moral obligation* to avoid suicide *as such,* an obligation, of course, which might be overridden by other obligations in some or many cases? (Captain Oates may have had a moral obligation not to commit suicide as such, but his obligation not to stand in the way of his comrades getting to safety might have been so strong that, everything considered, he was justified in leaving the polar camp and allowing himself to freeze to death.)

To present all the arguments necessary to answer this question convincingly would take a great deal of space. I shall, therefore, simply state one answer to it which seems plausible to some contemporary philosophers. Suppose it could be shown that it would maximize the long-run welfare of everybody affected if people were taught that there is a moral obligation to avoid suicide—so that people would be motivated to avoid suicide just because they thought it wrong (would have anticipatory guilt feelings at the very idea), and so that other people would be inclined to disapprove of persons who commit suicide unless there were some excuse (such as those mentioned in the first section). One might ask: how could it maximize utility to mold the conceptual and motivational structure of persons in this way? To which the answer might be: feeling in this way might make persons who are impulsively inclined to commit suicide in a bad mood, or a fit of anger or jealousy, take more time to deliberate; hence, some suicides that have bad effects generally might be prevented. In other words, it might be a good thing in its effects for people to feel about suicide in the way they feel about breach of promise or injuring others, just as it might be a good thing for people to feel a moral obligation not to smoke, or to wear seat belts. However, it might be that negative moral feelings about suicide as such would stand in the way of action by those persons whose welfare really is best served by suicide and whose suicide is the best thing for everybody concerned.

WHEN A DECISION TO COMMIT SUICIDE IS RATIONAL FROM THE PERSON'S POINT OF VIEW

The person who is contemplating suicide is obviously making a choice between future world-courses; the world-course that includes his demise, say, an hour from now, and several possible ones that contain his demise at a later point. One cannot have precise knowledge about many features of the latter group of world-courses, but it is certain that they will all end with death some (possibly short) finite time from now.

Why do I say the choice is between *world*-courses and not just a choice between future life-courses of the prospective suicide, the one shorter than the other? The reason is that one's suicide has some impact on the world (and one's continued life has some impact on the world), and that conditions in the rest of the world will often make a difference in one's evaluation of the possibilities. One *is* interested in things in the world other than just oneself and one's own happiness.

The basic question a person must answer, in order to determine which world-course is best or rational for him to choose, is which he *would* choose under conditions of optimal use of information, when *all* of his desires are taken into account. It is not just a question of what we prefer *now,* with some clarification of all the possibilities being considered. Our preferences change, and the preferences of tomorrow (assuming we can know something about them) are just as legitimately taken into account in deciding what to do now as the preferences of today. Since any reason that can be given today for weighting heavily today's preference can be given tomorrow for weighting heavily tomorrow's preference, the preferences of any time-stretch have a rational claim to an equal vote. Now the importance of that fact is this: we often know quite well that our desires, aversions, and preferences may change after a short while. When a person is in a state of despair—perhaps brought about by a rejection in love or discharge from a long-held position—nothing but the thing he cannot have seems desirable; everything else is turned to ashes. Yet we know quite well that the passage of time is likely to reverse all this; replacements may be found or other types of things that are available to us may begin to look attractive. So, if we were to act on the preferences of today alone, when the emotion of despair seems more than we can stand, we might find death preferable to life; but if we allow for the preferences of the weeks and years ahead, when many goals will be enjoyable and attractive, we might find life much preferable to death. So, if a choice of what is best is to be determined by what we want not only now but later (and later desires on an equal basis with the present ones)—as it should be—then what is the best or preferable world-course will often be quite different from what it would be if the choice, or what is best for one, were fixed by one's desires and preferences now.

Of course, if one commits suicide there are no future desires or aversions that may be compared with present ones and that should be allowed an equal vote in deciding what is best. In that respect the course of action that results in death is different from any other course of action we may undertake. I do not wish to suggest the rosy possibility that it is often or always reasonable to believe that next week "I shall be more interested in living than I am today, if today I take a dim view of continued existence." On the contrary, when a person is seriously ill, for instance, he may have no reason to think that the preference-order will be reversed —it may be that tomorrow he will prefer death to life more strongly.

The argument is often used that one can never be *certain* what is going to happen, and hence one is never rationally justified in doing anything as drastic as committing suicide. But we always have to live by probabilities and make our estimates as best we can. As soon as it is clear beyond reasonable doubt not only that death is now preferable to life, but also that it will be every day from now until the end, the rational thing is to act promptly.

Let us not pursue the question of whether it is rational for a person with a painful terminal illness to commit suicide; it is. However, the issue seldom arises, and few terminally ill patients do commit suicide. With such patients matters usually get worse slowly so that no particular time seems to call for action. They are often so heavily sedated that it is impossible for the mental processes of decision leading to action to occur; or else they are incapacitated in a hospital and the very physical possibility of ending their lives is not available. Let us leave this grim topic and turn to a practically more important problem: whether it is rational for persons to commit suicide for some reason other than painful terminal physical illness. Most persons who commit suicide do so, apparently, because they face a nonphysical problem that depresses them beyond their ability to bear.

Among the problems that have been regarded as good and sufficient reasons for ending life, we find (in addition to serious illness) the following: some event that has made a person feel ashamed or lose his prestige and status; reduction from affluence to poverty; the loss of a limb or of physical beauty; the loss of sexual capacity; some event that makes it seem impossible to achieve things by which one sets store; loss of a loved one; disappointment in love; the infirmities of increasing age. It is not to be denied that such things can be serious blows to a person's prospects of happiness.

Whatever the nature of an individual's problem, there are various plain errors to be avoided—errors to which a person is especially prone when he is depressed—in deciding whether, everything considered, he prefers a world-course containing his early demise to one in which his life continues to its natural terminus. Let us forget for a moment the relevance to the decision of preferences that he may have tomorrow, and concentrate on some errors that may infect his preference as of today, and for which correction or allowance must be made.

In the first place, depression, like any severe emotional experience, tends to primitivize one's intellectual processes. It restricts the range of one's survey of the possibilities. One thing that a rational person would do is compare the world-course containing his suicide with his *best* alternative. But his best alternative is precisely a possibility he may overlook if, in a depressed mood, he thinks only of how badly off he is and cannot imagine any way of improving his situation. If a person is disappointed in love, it is possible to adopt a vigorous plan of action that carries a good chance of acquainting him with someone he likes at least as well; and if old age prevents a person from continuing the tennis game with his favorite partner, it is possible to learn some other game that provides the joys of competition without the physical demands.

Depression has another insidious influence on one's planning; it seriously affects one's judgment about probabilities. A person disappointed in love is very likely to take a dim view of himself, his prospects, and his attractiveness; he thinks that because he has been rejected by one person he will probably be rejected by anyone who looks desirable to him. In a less gloomy frame of mind he would make different estimates. Part of the reason for such gloomy probability estimates is that depression tends to repress one's memory of evidence that supports a nongloomy prediction. Thus, a rejected lover tends to forget any cases in which he has elicited enthusiastic response from ladies in relation to whom he has been the one who has done the rejecting. Thus his pessimistic self-image is based upon a highly selected, and pessimistically selected, set of data. Even when he is reminded of the data, moreover, he is apt to resist an optimistic inference.

Another kind of distortion of the look of future prospects is not a result of depression, but is quite normal. Events distant in the future feel small, just as objects distant in space look small. Their prospect does not have the effect on motivational processes that it would have if it were of an event in the immediate future. Psychologists call this the "goal-gradient" phenomenon; a rat, for instance, will run faster toward a perceived food box than a distant unseen one. In the case of a person who has suffered some misfortune, and whose situation now is an unpleasant one, this reduction of the motivational influence of events distant in time has the effect that present unpleasant states weigh far more heavily than probable future pleasant ones in any choice of world-courses.

If we are trying to determine whether we now prefer, or shall later prefer, the outcome of one world-course to that of another (and this is leaving aside the questions of the weight of the votes of preferences at a later date), we must take into account these and other infirmities of our "sensing" machinery. Since knowing that the machinery is out of order will not tell us what results it would give if it were working, the best recourse might be to refrain from making any decision in a stressful frame of mind. If decisions have to be made, one must recall past reactions, in a normal frame of mind, to outcomes like those under assessment. But many suicides seem to occur in moments of despair. What should be clear from the above is that a moment of despair, if one is seriously contemplating suicide, ought to be a moment of reassessment of one's goals and values, a reassessment which the individual must realize is very difficult to make objectively, because of the very quality of his depressed frame of mind.

A decision to commit suicide may in certain circumstances be a rational one. But a person who wants to act rationally must take into account the various possible "errors" and make appropriate rectification of his initial evaluations.

THE ROLE OF OTHER PERSONS

What is the moral obligation of other persons toward those who are contemplating suicide? The question of their moral blameworthiness may be ignored and what is rational for them to do from the point of view of personal welfare may be considered as being of secondary concern. Laws make it dangerous to aid or encourage a suicide. The risk of running afoul of the law may partly determine moral obligation, since moral obligation to do something may be reduced by the fact that it is personally dangerous.

The moral obligation of other persons toward one who is contemplating suicide is an instance of a general obligation to render aid to those in serious distress, at least when this can be done at no great cost to one's self. I do not think this general principle is seriously questioned by anyone, whatever his moral theory; so I feel free to assume it as a premise. Obviously the person contemplating suicide is in great distress of some sort; if he were not, he would not be seriously considering terminating his life.

How great a person's obligation is to one in distress depends on a number of factors. Obviously family and friends have special obligations to devote time to helping the prospective suicide—which others do not have. But anyone in this kind of distress has a moral claim on the time of any person who knows the situation (unless there are others more responsible who are already doing what should be done).

What is the obligation? It depends, of course, on the situation, and how much the second person knows about the situation. If the individual has decided to terminate his life if he can, and it is clear that he is right in this decision, then, if he needs help in executing the decision, there is a moral obligation to give him help. On this matter a patient's physician has a special obligation, from which any talk about the Hippocratic oath does not absolve him. It is true that there are some damages one cannot be expected to absorb, and some risks which one cannot be expected to take, on account of the obligation to render aid.

On the other hand, if it is clear that the individual should not commit suicide, from the point of view of his own welfare, or if there is a presumption that he should not (when the only evidence is that a person is discovered unconscious, with the gas turned on), it would seem to be the individual's obligation to intervene, prevent the successful execution of the decision, and see to the availability of competent psychiatric advice and temporary hospitalization, if necessary. Whether one has a right to take such steps when a clearly sane person, after careful reflection over a period of time, comes to the conclusion that an end to his life is what is best for him and what he wants, is very doubtful, even when one thinks his conclusion a mistaken one; it would seem that a man's own considered decision about whether he wants to live must command respect, although one must concede that this could be debated.

The more interesting role in which a person may be cast, however, is that of adviser. It is often important to one who is contemplating suicide to go over his thinking with another, and to feel that a conclusion, one way or the other, has the support of a respected mind. One thing one can obviously do, in rendering the service of advice, is to discuss with the person the various types of issues discussed above, made more specific by the concrete circumstances of his case, and help him find whether, in view, say, of the damage his suicide would do to others, he has a moral obligation to refrain, and whether it is rational or best for him, from the point of view of his own welfare, to take this step or adopt some other plan instead.

To get a person to see what is the rational thing to do is no small job. Even to get a person, in a frame of mind when he is seriously contemplating (or perhaps has already unsuccessfully attempted) suicide, to recognize a plain truth of fact may be a major operation. If a man insists, "I am a complete failure," when it is obvious that by any reasonable standard he is far from that, it may be tremendously difficult to get him to see the fact. But there is another job beyond that of getting a person to see what is the rational thing to do; that is to help him *act* rationally, or *be* rational, when he has conceded what would be the rational thing.

How either of these tasks may be accomplished effectively may be discussed more competently by an experienced psychiatrist than by a philosopher. Loneliness and the absence of human affection are states which exacerbate any other problems; disappointment, reduction to poverty, and so forth, seem less impossible to bear in the presence of the affection of another. Hence simply to be a friend, or to find someone a friend, may be the largest contribution one can make either to helping a person be rational or see clearly what is rational for him to do; this service may make one who was contemplating suicide feel that there is a future for him which it is possible to face.

NOTES

1. Immanuel Kant, *Lectures on Ethics,* New York: Harper Torchbook (1963), p. 150 [see this volume, chapter 4, p. 49].

2. See St. Thomas Aquinas, *Summa Theologica,* Second Part of the Second Part, Q. 64, Art. 5 [chapter 2 of this volume]. In Article 7, he says: "Nothing hinders one act from having two effects, only one of which is intended, while the other is beside the intention. Now moral acts take their species according to what is intended, and not according to what is beside the intention, since this is accidental as explained above" (Q. 43, Art. 3: I–II, Q. 1, Art. 3, as 3). Mr. Norman St. John-Stevas, the most articulate contemporary defender of the Catholic view, writes as follows: "Christian thought allows certain exceptions to its general condemnation of suicide. That covered by a particular divine inspiration has already been noted. Another exception arises where suicide is the method imposed by the State for the execution of a just death penalty. A third exception is *altruistic* suicide, of which the best known example is Captain Oates. Such suicides are justified by invoking the principles of double effect. The act from which death results must be good or at least morally indifferent; some other good effect must result: The death must not be directly intended or the real means to the good effect: and a grave reason must exist for adopting the course of action" [*Life, Death and the Law* (Bloomington, Ind.: Indiana University Press, 1961), pp. 250–51]. Presumably the Catholic doctrine is intended to allow suicide when this is required for meeting strong moral obligations; whether it can do so consistently depends partly on the interpretation given to "real means to the good effect." Readers interested in pursuing further the Catholic doctrine of double effect and its implications for our problem should read Philippa Foot, "The Problem of Abortion and the Doctrine of Double Effect," *The Oxford Review* 5 (1967): 5–15.

3. R. B. Brandt, *Ethical Theory* (Englewood Cliffs, N.J.: Prentice-Hall, 1959), pp. 61–82.

4. John Locke, *Two Treatises of Government,* ch. 2.

5. Kant, *Lectures on Ethics,* p. 154 [see this volume, chapter 4, p. 52].

6. This essay appears in collections of Hume's works [see chapter 3 in this volume].

7. For an argument similar to Kant's, see also St. Thomas Aquinas, *Summa Theologica,* II, II, Q. 64, Art. 5 [chapter 2 in this volume].

8. Immanuel Kant, *The Fundamental Principles of the Metaphysic of Morals,* trans. H. J. Paton (London: The Hutchinson Group, 1948), ch. 2.

9. Aristotle, *Nicomachaean Ethics,* Bk. 5, Ch. 10, p. 1138a.

10. St. Thomas Aquinas, *Summa Theologica,* II, II, Q. 64, Art. 5 [see this volume, chapter 2, p. 34].

11. Sir William Blackstone, *Commentaries,* 4:189; Brown in *Hales* v. *Petit,* I Plow, 253, 75 E.R. 387 (C.B. 1563). Both cited by Norman St. John-Stevas, *Life, Death, and the Law,* p. 235.

16

On Choosing Death

Philip E. Devine

A celebrated Epicurean argument runs as follows: since death is annihilation, since (in Aristotle's phrase) "nothing is thought to be any longer good or bad for the dead,"[1] it follows not that death is the greatest of all evils but that death is no evil at all. Fear of death is irrational, because there is nothing of the appropriate sort—no state or condition of ourselves as conscious beings—to be afraid of in death.[2] This Epicurean argument supports the common contention that death may sometimes be an object of rational choice.

I wish to discuss critically this view, and to attempt to support the claim (for which the testimony of sensitive persons is overwhelming) that there is something uncanny about death, especially one's own.[3] I do not want to deny that a suicide can be calmly and deliberately, and in that sense rationally, carried out. But then someone might calmly and deliberately do something blatantly foolish or even pointless, and it is sometimes rational to act quickly and with passionate fervor. But if, as seems plausible, a precondition of rational choice is that one know *what* one is choosing, either by experience or by the testimony of others who have

From *The Ethics of Homicide* (Ithaca, N.Y.: Cornell University Press, 1978), pp. 138–43. Reprinted with the permission of the author.

experienced it or something very like it, then it is not possible to choose death rationally. Nor is any degree of knowledge of what one desires to escape by death helpful, since rational choice between two alternatives requires knowledge of both. The issue is not whether pain (say) is bad, but whether a certain degree of pain is worse than death. It might seem at least that progressively more intense misery gives progressively stronger reasons for killing oneself, but the situation is rather like this. If one is heating a metal whose melting point one does not know at all, one knows that the more heat one applies, the closer one gets to melting the metal. But it does not follow that it is possible to know—before the metal actually starts melting—that one has even approached the melting point.

It is necessary, however, seriously to consider the contention that there are experiences—being flayed and kept alive by ingenious means afterwards for instance—in preference to which it is clearly rational to choose death. At this point in the argument it is necessary to separate the claim that such a choice would be rationally required (that it would not be rational to decide to continue to live under such circumstances) from the claim that it is rationally permitted (that it might be rational both to decide to live and to decide to die). As far as the first of these possibilities is concerned, I do not see how someone could be considered irrational if he decides to show what a human being is capable of enduring. As for the second, while it is true that suicide under such circumstances has a powerful appeal, so does suicide in many other circumstances as well, such as when one will otherwise be exposed to disgrace and dishonor of an extreme sort, or when one is convinced that one's unbearable emotional difficulties will never be resolved. Perhaps all these kinds of suicide are rational too (although contemporary defenders of the possibility of rational suicide do not commonly think so), but if so their rationality is not of the calculative sort. We are dealing, that is, not with a situation concerning which rational men will exhibit a range of estimates, but with a situation in which one man's estimate is as good as another, because what is being done is a comparison with an unknown quality.

I do not mean to imply that we can have no knowledge of what death is, that we cannot for instance teach a child the meaning of "death." But consider what we can do. We can show the child a corpse, but a corpse is not a dead person (that is, not in the required sense of something which is dead and a person, something one of us—except in a stretched sense—could be), but only what a person leaves behind when he dies. We can make the child a witness at a deathbed, but to do that is simply to show a living person becoming a corpse. We can tell the child that death is not seeing friends any more (and so on), but somehow he will have to learn how to take these negatives properly, since otherwise death will be confused with all one's friends' leaving town. Finally, we can tell him a myth, even a subdued one such as "death is everlasting sleep," or that death is the absence of life, much as nakedness is the absence of clothing. (In nakedness, of course, the person who existed clothed continues to exist unclothed.) And that such mythology is logically appropriate is part of what I shall call the opaqueness of death.

The opaqueness of death does not result from uncertainty as to our condition afterward, although what I am getting at is sometimes expressed in such terms. My point is rather that it is folly to think that one can housebreak death by representing it as annihilation. One might—considering that the opaqueness of death is a *logical* opaqueness—be tempted to compare the qualms I have expressed about rationally choosing death with skeptical qualms about our right to believe that the sun will rise tomorrow, which rest on the logical difference between inductive and deductive reasoning. To press this comparison would be a mistake, however, for two reasons. First, we routinely have to make choices based on inductive evidence, whereas we do not routinely choose to die or to go on living. Second, the myths cited indicate that the opaqueness of death is a real element in human motivation and self-understanding, an element that cannot be neglected even, or especially, if one considers these myths all to be false.

Human beings characteristically find themselves in profound imaginative and intellectual difficulty when they attempt to envisage the end of their existence. This difficulty is not lessened by the experience of sleep, since sleep, even when dreamless, presupposes the continuation of the self in being and the possibility of an awakening. (I say the possibility, since someone might die before he wakes, and Sleeping Beauty remains alive though asleep even if Prince Charming never arrives.) Nor is the difficulty lessened by interviewing those whose hearts have stopped and who have revived, since what one would learn about in that way is not death but apparent dying.

The difficulty does not lie, at least not centrally, in imagining a world without me, but rather in connecting this world with my (self-regarding) concerns. (Altruistic and disinterested concerns are not at issue at this particular point, since they do not bear on the question of why death can be an evil for the dead person himself. In any case, an altruistic suicide can be rational or irrational in a straightforward way: I might be rational in believing that my suicide will protect my comrades from the secret police, whereas if I lived I would talk and they would be captured and tortured to death, and I might be quite unrealistic in my calculation of the effect my self-immolation will have on public opinion.) Even my aversions, my desires not to experience certain things, do not connect easily with such a world, since there is for instance a logical gap between "freedom from pain" resulting from the nonexistence of the subject of pain and ordinary painless existence. To put the point another way, if I am contemplating suicide, I am not trying to choose (not centrally, that is) "between future world-courses: the world-course which contains my demise, say, an hour from now, and several possible ones which contain my demise at a later point."[4] What I am contemplating is much more intimate than a world-course. It is my own (self-chosen) death, and such a choice presents itself inevitably as a leap in the dark.

But the decision to kill oneself—it might be argued—need not reflect a preference of death over life, but rather of one (shorter) life over another, or of one (speedier) death over another. The clearest cases of preferences of this sort are choices it would be odd to call suicide. I might take a remedy that makes my present life more tolerable, while somewhat shortening its length, or I might, being tied up and about to be hanged, decide to jump rather than wait to be pushed. Self-execution is in a class apart from ordinary suicide in any case, as any reader of the *Phaedo* might confirm, and it may be possible to speak of self-execution even in cases where the person convicted does what the executioner ought to do, and commutes, with his own hand, a painful and degrading death to one that is relatively painless. The distinction between choosing death rather than life and choosing one kind of life or death rather than another does not turn, in any case, on the nearness of the death in question. A remedy that makes present life more tolerable may shorten a life expectancy of forty years to thirty-five, or of a week to a day. And if a twenty-year-old should choose irrevocably to be killed at seventy, it would, I think, be fair to say that he had chosen death (at seventy) in preference to old age.

One can perhaps get a better grip on what is involved here by comparing the choice of death with other radical and irreversible choices. (Some first-time choices, e.g., to visit London, present no problem, since one knows that one can always cut one's losses if things do not turn out as desired.) In many of these choices one can be guided, in part at any rate, by the experience of those who have gone before, but this will not always work, since there had to be a first person to undergo a sex-change operation, take LSD, and so on. Choices of this sort are not necessarily irrational, but if rational . . . their rationality must be explained in terms of the general rationality of risk-taking (which is supported to a degree by experience). This notion does not seem to apply in the case of choosing death. The difference between these choices and that of death is a logical one. While it is logically possible (even if not possible in this particular case) to get an idea of what it is like to have taken LSD, from someone who has done so, death is of necessity that from which no one returns to give tidings.

One might, indeed, attempt to explain our fear of death in precisely these terms: fear of death is fear of the unknown. Of course this is a metaphor, since the opaqueness of death is logical rather than epistemological. But the unknown is attractive as well as fearful, and death has in fact, alongside its fearfulness, the attractiveness which is a feature of the limits of human experience. It does not seem possible, on these premises alone, to resolve the tension between death's fearfulness and its attractiveness.

NOTES

1. *Nicomachean Ethics* 1115a 25, trans. W. D. Ross, in Richard McKeon, ed., *The Basic Works of Aristotle* (New York: Random House, 1941), p. 975.

2. Lucretius, *De Rerum Natura,* III, 870 ff.

3. I'd like to discuss these, that is, without falling into the logical errors criticized by someone like Paul Edwards. See his article "My Death," in Paul Edwards, ed., *Encyclopedia of Philosophy* (New York, 1967), vol. 5.

4. Richard B. Brandt, "The Morality and Rationality of Suicide," p. 117 [see this volume, chapter 15, p. 193].

17

The Art of Suicide

Joyce Carol Oates

In the morning of life the son tears himself loose from the mother, from the domestic hearth, to rise through battle to his destined heights. Always he imagines his worst enemy in front of him, yet he carries the enemy within himself—a deadly longing for the abyss, a longing to drown in his own source, to be sucked down to the realm of the Mothers. His life is a constant struggle against extinction, a violent yet fleeting deliverance from ever-lurking night. This death is no external enemy, it is his own inner longing for the stillness and profound peace of all-knowing non-existence, for all-seeing sleep in the ocean of coming-to-be and passing away.

C. G. Jung, *Symbols of Transformation*

Not only the artist, that most deliberate of persons, but all human beings employ metaphor: the conscious or unconscious creation of concrete, lit-

Joyce Carol Oates, "The Art of Suicide," in *The Reevaluation of Existing Values and the Search for Absolute Values. Proceedings of the Seventh International Conference on the Unity of the Sciences* (New York: International Cultural Foundation Press, 1978), pp. 183–90. Reprinted by permission. Excerpt from "Lady Lazarus" in *Ariel* by Sylvia Plath. Copyright © 1961, 1962, 1963, 1964, 1965 by Ted Hughes. Printed in England by Faber & Faber as *Collected Poems,* copyright Ted Hughes 1965, 1981. Reprinted by permission of Harper & Row, Publishers, Inc., and Olwyn Hughes. Excerpt from "Waiting to Die" from *Live or Die* by Anne Sexton. Copyright © 1966 by Anne Sexton. Reprinted by permission of Houghton Mifflin Company.

eral terms that seek to express the abstract, the not-at-hand, the ineffable. Is the suicide an artist? Is Death-by-Suicide an art form, the employment of a metaphor so vast, so final, that it obliterates and sweeps into silence all opposition? But there are many suicides, there are many deaths, some highly conscious and others groping, perplexed, perhaps murderous, hardly conscious at all: a succumbing to the gravitational pull of which Jung speaks in the quotation above, which takes him away from the "realm of the Mothers"—but only for a while, until his life's energy runs its course, and he is drawn down into what Jung calls, in metaphorical language that is beautiful, even seductive, the "profound peace of all-knowing non-existence." Yet if we were to push aside metaphor, if we were no longer even to speak in a reverential tone of Death, but instead of Deadness —mere, brute, blunt, flat, distinctly unseductive Deadness—how artistic a venture is it, how meaningfully can it engage our deepest attention?

My thesis is a simple one: apart from circumstances which insist upon self-destruction as the inevitable next move, the necessary next move that will preserve one's dignity, the act of suicide itself is a consequence of the employment of false metaphors. It is a consequence of the atrophying of the creative imagination: the failure of the imagination, not to be confused with gestures or freedom, or rebellion, or originality, or transcendence. To so desperately confuse the terms of our finite contract as to invent a liberating Death when it is really brute, inarticulate Deadness that awaits—the "artist" of suicide is a groping, blundering, failed artist, and his art-work a mockery of genuine achievement.

The "artistic" suicide—in contrast to the suicide who acts in order to hasten an inevitable end, perhaps even to alleviate terrible pain—is always mesmerized by the imaginative act of self-destruction, *as if it were a kind of creation*. It is a supreme gesture of the will, an insistence upon one's absolute freedom; that it is "contrary to nature," a dramatic violation of the life-force, makes the gesture all the more unique. One can determine one's self, one's identity, by choosing to put an end to that identity—which is to say, an end to finitude itself. The suicide who deliberates over his act, who very likely has centered much of his life around the possibility of the act, rejects our human condition of finitude (all that we are not, as well as all that we are); his self-destruction is a disavowal, in a sense, of what it means to *be* human. But does the suicide who is transfixed by metaphor suffer a serious derangement of perception, so that he contemplates the serene, transcendental, Platonic "all-knowing non-existence" while what awaits him is merely a biological death—that is, deadness?

In Sylvia Plath's famous poem "Lady Lazarus" the young woman poet boasts of her most recent suicide attempt in language that, though carefully restrained by the rigorous formal discipline of the poem, strikes us as very close to hysteria. She is a "smiling woman," only thirty; and like the cat she has nine times to die. (Though in fact Plath's next attempt, an attempt said not to have been altogether serious, was to be her last.) She is clearly proud of herself, though self-mocking as well, and her angry contempt for the voyeurs crowding around is beautifully expressed:

> What a million filaments.
> The peanut-crunching crowd
> Shoves in to see
>
> Them unwind me hand and foot—
> The big strip tease.
> Gentlemen, ladies
>
> These are my hands
> My knees
> I may be skin and bone,
>
> Nevertheless, I am the same, identical woman.
>
> Dying
> Is an art, like everything else.
> I do it exceptionally well.
> I do it so it feels like hell.
> I do it so it feels real.
> I guess you could say I've a call.

In this poem and in numerous others from the collections *Ariel* and *Winter Trees* the poet creates vivid images of self-loathing, frequently projected onto other people or onto nature, and consequently onto life itself. It is Sylvia Plath whom Sylvia Plath despises, and by confusing her personality with the deepest layer of being, her own soul, she makes self-destruction inevitable. It is not *life* that has become contaminated, and requires a radical exorcism; it is the temporal personality, the smiling thirty-year-old woman trapped in a failing marriage and overburdened with the responsibilities of motherhood, in one of the coldest winters in

England's recorded history. Unable to strike out at her ostensible enemies (her husband Ted Hughes, who had left her for another woman; her father, long dead, who had "betrayed" her by dying when she was a small child), Plath strikes out at the enemy within, and murders herself in her final shrill poems before she actually turns on the gas oven and commits suicide. If her death, and even many of her poems, strike us as adolescent gestures it is perhaps because she demonstrated so little self-knowledge; her anguish was sheer emotion, never translated into coherent images. Quite apart from the surreal figures of speech Plath employs with such frenzied power, her work exhibits a curious deficiency of imagination, most evident in the autobiographical novel *The Bell Jar,* in which the suicidal narrator speaks of her consciousness as trapped inside a bell-jar, forced to breathe again and again the same stale air.

"There is but one truly serious philosophical question," Camus has said in a statement now famous, "and that is suicide." Camus exaggerates, certainly, and it is doubtful whether, strictly speaking, suicide is a "philosophical" problem at all. It may be social, moral, even economic, even political—especially political; but is it "philosophical"? Marcus Aurelius noted in his typically prudent manner: "In all that you do or say or think, recollect that at any time the power of withdrawal from life is in your hands," and Nietzsche said, perhaps less somberly, "The thought of suicide is a strong consolation; one can get through many a bad night with it." But these are *problems,* these are *thoughts;* that they are so clearly conceptualized suggests their detachment from the kind of anguish, raw and undifferentiated, that drove Sylvia Plath to her premature death. The poet Anne Sexton liked to claim that suicides were a special people. "Talking death" for suicides is "life." In Sexton's third collection of poems, *Live or Die,* she included a poem characterized by remarkable restraint and dignity, one of the most intellectual (and despairing) works of what is loosely called the "confessional mode." Is suicide a philosophical problem? Is it intellectual, abstract, cerebral? Hardly:

> Since you ask, most days I cannot remember.
> I walk in my clothing, unmarked by that voyage.
> Then the almost unnameable lust returns.
>
> For then I have nothing against life.
> I know well the grass blades you mention,
> the furniture you have placed under the sun.

But suicides have a special language.
Like carpenters they want to know *which tools*.
They never ask *why build*.

In Sexton the gravitational pull toward death seems to preclude, or exclude, such imaginative speculations as those of Camus; *that* death is desirable is never questioned.

Of course there are the famous suicides, the noble suicides, who do not appear to have been acting blindly, out of a confused emotional state: there is Socrates who acquiesced courteously, who did not choose to flee his execution; there is Cato; Petronius; Jesus of Nazareth. In literature there are, famously, Shakespeare's Othello, who *rises* to his death, and Shakespeare's Antony and Cleopatra, both of whom outwit their conquerors by dying, the latter an "easy" death, the former an awkward, ghastly Roman death, poorly executed. Macbeth's ferocious struggle with Macduff is a suicidal gesture, and a perfect one, as is Hamlet's final combat with the enemy most like himself in age and spirit. The Hamlet-like Stavrogin of Dostoyevsky's monumental *The Possessed* worries that he may lack the "magnanimity" to kill himself, and to rid the world of such a loathsome creature as he; but he acquires the necessary strength and manages to hang himself, a symbolic gesture tied up clearly with Dostoyevsky's instinct for the logic of self-destruction as a consequence of modern man's "freedom" (i.e., alienation) from his nation.

Is the subjective act, then, nursed and groomed and made to bring forth its own sort of sickly fruit, really a public, political act? "Many die too late, and a few die too early," Nietzsche says boldly. "The doctrine still sounds strange: *Die at the right time!*" Nietzsche does not address himself to the less-than-noble; he is speaking, perhaps, not to individuals at all but to trans-individual values that, once healthy, are now fallen into decay, and must be hastened to their inevitable historical end. If until recent times death has been a taboo subject in our culture, suicide has been nothing short of an obscenity: a sudden raucous jeering shout in a genteel gathering. The suicide does not play the game, does not observe the rules; he leaves the party too soon, and leaves the other guests painfully uncomfortable. The world which has struck them as tolerable, or even enjoyable, is, perhaps to a more discerning temperament, simply impossible: like Dostoyevsky's Ivan Karamazov, he respectfully returns his ticket to his Creator. The private gesture becomes violently and unmistakably public, which accounts for the harsh measures taken to punish suicides—or the bodies of suicides—over the centuries.

It is possible to reject society's extreme judgment, I think, without taking up an unqualified cause for the "freedom" of suicide, particularly if one makes sharp distinctions between kinds of suicides—the altruistic, the pathological, and the metaphorical. It is in metaphorical self-murder that what is murdered is an aspect of the self, and what is attained is a fictitious "transcendence" of physical circumstance.

But can one freely choose a condition, a state of being, that has never been experienced except in the imagination and, even there, *only in metaphor?* The wish "I want to die" might be a confused statement masking any number of unarticulated wishes: "I want to punish you, and you, and you"; "I want to punish the loathsome creature that appears to be myself"; "I want to be taken up by my Creator, and returned to the bliss of my first home"; "I want to alter my life because it is so disappointing, or painful, or boring"; "I want to silence the voices that are always shouting instructions"; "I want—I know not what." Rationally one cannot "choose" Death because Death is an unknown experience, and perhaps it isn't even an "experience"—perhaps it is simply nothing; and one cannot imagine nothing. The brain simply cannot fathom it, however glibly its thought-clusters may verbalize *nonexistence, negation of being, Death,* and other nonreferential terms. There is a curious heckling logic to the suicide's case, but his initial premise may be totally unfounded. *I want to die* may in fact be an empty statement expressing merely an emotion: *I am terribly unhappy at the present time.*

Still, people commit suicide because it is their deepest, most secret wish, and if the wish is too secret to be consciously admitted it will manifest itself in any number of metaphorical ways. We can list some of them—alcoholism, accidents, self-induced malnutrition, wretched life-choices, a cultivation of melancholy. The world is there, the world *is,* not awaiting our interpretations but unresisting when we compose them, and it may be that the mere semblance of the world's acquiescence to our metaphor-making leads us deeper and deeper into illusion. Because passion, even misdirected and self-pitying and claustrophobic, is always appealing, and has the power to drown out quieter, more reasonable voices, we will always be confronted by the fascination an intelligent public will feel for the most skillfully articulated of death-wishes.